make more money, roc

money, roc

your career, an

revel in your

individualit

→ make more money

rock your career,

nd revel in ←

your individualit

make more money.

rock your caree

RULES
FOR RENEGADES

RULES
FOR RENEGADES

how to
make more money,
rock your career,
and revel in your
individuality

CHRISTINE
COMAFORD-LYNCH

McGraw-Hill

New York   Chicago   San Francisco
Lisbon   London   Madrid   Mexico City   Milan
New Delhi   San Juan   Seoul   Singapore
Sydney   Toronto

1 2 3 4 5 6 7 8 9 0   DOC/DOC   0 9 8 7

ISBN-13: 978-0-07-148975-1
ISBN-10:   0-07-148975-4

Design by Mauna Eichner and Lee Fukui

I'm in my forties. My memory isn't what it used to be. Some of the dates
I've stated may be off by a few months or even a year. Except for the
famous people, most other names have been changed, along with identifying characteristics in a few cases. In the event that a living person actually does resemble one of the nonfamous people I mention in this book,
that's one heck of a coincidence, and not what I intended. For brevity,
there are a few composite characters. The advice, ideas, and techniques
in this book have worked for me. They may not work for you. I trust you
understand that.

For my husband, Chris Lynch,
my favorite renegade.

CONTENTS

PREFACE

You're a renegade—you have a level of passion and commitment that others don't. You're apt to break the rules that are blocking you from getting things done. You're a renegade because you want to build something great, have a fulfilling career, and not be required to sacrifice yourself on the altar of success. Whether you are (or want to be) an entrepreneur leading your own company or an intrapreneur within someone else's, whether the company is large or small, for profit or not, it doesn't matter. Maybe you're even returning to the workforce or heading into it for the first time. I know how it feels because I was a renegade too, whether I knew it or not.

My journey into the world of business never bulleted down the express lane. At age 16 I ran away to New York City to become a model. Six months later I talked my way into college without a high school diploma. Neither New York's fashion scene nor academia satisfied my yearning to make a difference in the world, so I became a Buddhist monk. At 24 I broke my vows. At 25 I got a burger, a boyfriend, and a bottom-rung job at Microsoft. I embraced my inner geek, but I also figured that the way to make my mark and help others was to start building companies. At 27 I decided to become a millionaire. Ten years later, I had made over $10 million and given $3 million of it away to assorted nonprofits. At 40 I retired, having consulted to 700 companies in the Fortune 1000 and hundreds of small businesses, created over 5,000 jobs, found the man of my dreams, got married, and became a stepmom to an incredible son.

Sounds fantastic, right? That's the stuff for the front page of the résumé. Here's the stuff that isn't exactly front-page news: I also screwed up royally. Lots of times. I lost sight of the good intentions that sent me into business in the first place. I gave power over my life away to other people again and again, letting them decide whether I was worthy enough. I chased after impossible standards of beauty, bleaching my dark hair blonde so aggressively that it broke off at the roots and I had to wear a wig for eight months. I fell in with a cult and almost ruined my hard-won reputation and business career digging myself out. I was so busy expanding my Rolodex that I blew off a bunch of great friends. I turned myself into such a molar-grinding, burned-out ball of anxiety that I needed a facelift at age 38 and had to have my teeth recapped at age 42. Oh, and did I mention that I made a little business mistake that cost me $8 million? It took some major wake-up calls—including, sadly, helping to care for my dying father—to get me back to the necessary work of reclaiming my life's purpose.

Today, at age 44, I'm still a work in progress. I've

rejoined the workforce with a job that feeds my soul: I help accelerate businesses, big and small, by showing people how to develop their inner entrepreneur. I write, deliver seminars and speeches, and am an active volunteer. I still mess up, but I do it less often and with a broader perspective.

Your path is different from mine, but I'm guessing we have some things in common. You want a fabulous life and career—maybe you have a vision that you want to make into a reality. You want to succeed without totally sacrificing your personal life. I wrote this book for you. Depending on where you are in your career, you may need what's in some of these chapters more immediately than others. Read them in the order you want. Ultimately you'll want to read them all, because there's something in every chapter that will be helpful. And if you skip some, you'll miss a lot of good stories.

This book is the distillation of what I've learned as I've succeeded (and failed) in business, built strong, loving relationships (and some disasters), and evolved in my spiritual life. I didn't start with any advantages—mega-brains, status, or money, for instance—so if I did it, anyone can. If you simply want to become financially independent, this book can help. If you want a meaningful life full of rich connections, this book can help. If you want to integrate spirituality with your work, this book can help. If you want to have more self-confidence and self-esteem, this book can help. If you want perfectly toned abs, killer buns, and thinner thighs in 30 days, sorry, this book can't help.

My plan was to show you how exhilarating and creative and kick-ass business can be by telling you a lot of funny stories about my career, so you could laugh and gasp as you read about the total triumphs and absolute train wrecks I've presided over. There's a lot to learn from both. But as I mulled over my life as an entrepreneur, I realized that there was a bigger story to tell—the hard-won wisdom that emerges from building a fulfilling life while rocking your career.

I'm guessing you love freebies as much as I do. I'll always treasure my hand towels from the White House (okay, maybe they didn't exactly *give* them to me). So I've filled this book with lots of cool free stuff: links to a sample business plan outline, tutorials on sales and marketing techniques, tools to help you build your own power and deal with rejection, and much, much more.

I hope you'll learn from my stories that the return on the investment in your career and life is worth a thousand times the cost. You'll gain power, courage, confidence, and optimism. You'll know that whatever challenges come your way, you'll emerge triumphant. You'll thrive, not simply survive. Okay, renegade, let's rock.

Christine Comaford-Lynch

Christine would love to visit your book club. Please email contact@mightyventures.com or call (707) 255-6246 to schedule a visit.

ACKNOWLEDGMENTS

This book wouldn't have come to be without the help of many people. First, my agent, Jim Levine of Levine Greenberg Literary Agency, believed in me even when I had no idea what I wanted to write. Thanks, Jim. Every author should wish for an agent as awesome as you.

Once I determined my literary direction, numerous dear friends ceaselessly read my chapters and commented on them in detail. I owe a whopping debt of gratitude to Chris Lynch, Laurie McLean, Casey Lynch, Geri Spieler, Christine Lee, Tim Miller, Carolyn Akel, Sanjiva Nath, Bonnie Durrance, Michele Ikemire, Len Foley, Rebecca Gauthier, Jonny Bowden, Ann Cash, Ann Mitchell, Anna Hess, Lee Meehan, Karen Baker, Ransom Stephens, and the fabulous Black Point Writers.

Additional thanks are due to the friends who egged me on in the early days, and read my far-from-polished prose: Marina McMillan, Bonnie Digrius, Jewel Savadelis, Koann Vikoren Skrzyniarz, Mary Camarata,

Maggie Berger, Dan Lynch, Jerry Jampolsky, Kamini Rangappan. Thanks, too, to the writing teachers who helped in my quest to find my story and voice: Linda Runyan, Adair Lara, Peter Richardson, Cate Merritt Murphy, and Paul Chutkow. Extra thanks to Paul for introducing me to the incomparable Walt Bode.

Walt Bode deserves heartfelt thanks for agonizing with me over chapter structure and order, and helping me to cut the fat from early drafts. You've got one sharp machete, Walt, and you know how to use it.

Thanks also to Debra Condren, my author-mentor, who told me what to expect and when. If you've not read Debra's book *AmBITCHous,* you should. She introduced me to Elizabeth "Betsy" Rapoport, the best book proposal writer I've ever met—and I've met tons. Thanks, Betsy, for helping me to see the light and embrace the direction this book needed to go.

Mary Glenn and the team at McGraw-Hill had the vision to see the potential of this book and were eager to take on the controversial and edgy nature of it. Thanks, everyone. And thanks in perpetuity for the massive marketing and publicity programs you have launched on this book's behalf!

A writer does not live on toner cartridge and electrons alone. Thanks to Dori Kirk and Esther Dungan for keeping the office together and preserving my sanity. Thanks to Dixie and the gang at Details, the best salon in Napa Valley. They graciously accommodated me through repeated reschedules, running lates, and last-minute appointments. Thanks also to Vinnie Fernandez, for making me work out on the days I begged to loll about in a copyediting-induced coma. Thanks to the team at the Center for Attitudinal Healing for providing me with countless opportunities for life-changing service.

My mentors and Senseis of the Day have taught me so much—and all by example. Without these extraordinary people I wouldn't have had the stories to tell you in this book. You know who you are.

The Lynch Clan, my exceptional gang of in-laws, has offered me continual support and encouragement along the way. Thanks for teaching me what a family looks like. I appreciate and love you all so very much.

I'll always be thankful to Joan Ziegler for reading my early work, being a dear friend and role model, and for introducing me to my husband. Speaking of husbands, Chris endured my obsession to make this book the best it could be. He also cheered me on as I took the risk to reveal my professional and personal flaws. Thanks, Honey.

My stepson, Spike (Francis), compassionate athlete-poet, has been a terrific sounding board. If you can't keep a 13-year-old engaged, the story must be edited . . . often significantly. Thanks for being straight with me, Spike. You always are.

My mom, Nancy Comaford, has put up with me all these years as I ran away and reinvented and finally returned home to help her through my dad's cancer.

Thanks for finding the humor in my wayward days and ways, Mom. Love you!

And last, thanks to my dad, the late great Carter Comaford. He showed me what an entrepreneur looks like and taught me that it's never too late to turn your life around. Never. Thanks, Dad.

Everything's an Illusion, So Pick One That's Empowering

Pulling a Company Out of Thin Air and Making a Few Million

*Reality is merely an illusion, albeit a
very persistent one.*

ALBERT EINSTEIN

RENEGADES DESIGN the right reality—both for themselves and for their companies. But what is reality? Are you sure? When I began my study of human potential in my teens, one of the oft-repeated refrains was the concept that everything is an illusion. I remember thinking, "Heck, if that's true, I can be anything!" When I say "illusion," I don't mean that everything is fake, like the *Matrix* world. I just mean that our lives are things we create ourselves by the way we think and feel. Shakespeare knew it too: "Nothing is but thinking makes it so." We create illusions every minute of every day at every stage of our lives. These illusions can be positive or negative, growth inducing or destructive. Only when we recognize our propensity to create our own reality can we do it consciously, fostering happy, progressive illusions instead of unhappy ones that hold us back.

Snap judgments happen all the time. You make them about others; others make them about you. First we need to change the judgments we make about ourselves. Then we can take on the judgments of others. We won't always be able to change them, but we will be able to apply our influence by offering others a more positive impression. Remember that our self-definition is an illusion—and often a rigid one.

Sometimes I've been totally psyched out by a new role I wanted to take. I've wrestled with self-doubt. *I don't have what it takes, I don't know the right people, I'm poor, I'm scared, I'm unpopular, I'm dweeby and lack social graces* . . . Do any of these sound familiar? This is fostering destructive illusions. Here's what I've learned: you will stay small, and your life will stay small, until you drop all that emotional baggage. Dumping baggage is hard work, and I don't want to minimize the challenge. Please forgive me if I proceed to give you a compassionate kick in the pants. I wasted a lot of time and energy battling these demons and would like to spare you the same suffering. Dump your baggage; abandon your destructive illusions. If you want to race toward your dreams, it helps to travel light.

Like most people's childhoods, mine wasn't perfect. When my dad told me that he wished I'd been a boy, and that as a girl I wasn't smart or pretty enough, I took it to heart, I embraced this destructive illusion, morphing by turns into a controller, rescuer, and manager. I was obsessed with proving my worth so I wouldn't get tossed out of the boat. It took me decades to figure out how to reframe things; my dad's criticisms were my motivation to find my own value, to convert pain to action to results. To a great extent, my self-sufficiency and skills for motivating others and accelerating businesses were born from my dad labeling me as deficient. I had to find my own worth, bring it forth, and show myself I had more value than I'd been told. And as I did, something supercool happened: over time I realized that my father didn't mean to discourage me at all—his intention was to toughen me up, to prepare me for the world. Eventually my father became a trusted advisor. *More often than not, our destructive illusions can be turned into something empowering.*

I believe that when we're born, we're all given exactly one unit of self-worth. No more, no less. No one can take it away; no one can add to it. Sometimes, though, we've forgotten we have it, and we need to recover it. Self-worth is a story, just like feeling unworthy is. So go ahead and declare yourself worthy. It's all an illusion anyway.

Twilight of the Dark Lord

The Human Resource Junior Executive. I'm sure you've run into this prototype. We have them at Microsoft, and the most tricky one has been a guy I'll call "Dick." Don't let his 20-something preppy look fool you. Beneath his navy jacket and khaki pants, beneath his Nordic beauty, he behaves as if he's the Dark Overlord of HR. But try as he may to wield his positional power over us, we contractors know we're 20 percent of the engineering workforce. He needs us.

When I pass him in the hallway, Dick greets me with my e-mail address, stressing my temporary status. "Hello, t dash chris c." His superior stance, his puppy snarl, his tiny bared teeth seem to say, "You may be here, but you're temporary: your e-mail starts with 't dash.'" Never mind that we share the fridge with the permanent employees, enjoy the eight different flavors of free juice, six varieties of free milk—the "t-" defines our rank.

Microsoft has hundreds of independent contractors—in programming, software testing, you name it. Many of us have worked here for years, and as defined by the IRS, we're actually employees. This means Microsoft should have been withholding taxes for us, but it hasn't. So the IRS is pissed off. Big time. They've hit Microsoft hard. It's 1989, and in Berlin the Wall is tumbling down; in Redmond, Washington, Microsoft's HR department is tottering too. I like when things are falling down, because if you move fast, you can grab something good.

Dick has summoned us contractors to the conference room for a mandatory meeting. "Attention . . . attention everyone, let's begin." Most of us continue talking softly, so Dick clears his throat and cranks up his volume. "At Microsoft, our policy is to employ top talent." Dick stands at the podium and nods at two young guys in blue suits standing to his right. "And if that talent won't be an employee, we've let it be an independent contractor. Until now." He pauses for impact, hoping the crowd of 300 will hold its collective breath, but our conversations continue. Dick's face is burning red. He hates that we don't respect him. "Bottom line, somebody needs to pay your taxes. To make sure that happens, you must become employees. Pronto."

The last thing we want is to be employees. We work for ourselves. We're making major bank here, clocking full pay for our 80-plus hours a week, making three times what the salaried employees make. Okay, so we don't have stock options or health benefits, but this company has been public for only a few years—it's still super-risky. Cash over Microsoft stock options? Any day. I may be young, but I'm not *stupid*.

"If you don't want to be a Microsoft employee—and I don't know who would pass up the opportunity—then Volt Technical Services will employ you." He nods to the two blue suits. They leer at us like hungry wolves. Why be pimped by a massive job shop? They'll take a huge cut from our paychecks for the "service" of withholding our income taxes. I'd rather service myself, thanks.

My former officemate, Dan, is next to me. He leans toward me, looks up through his stringy brown hair, fluorescent lights reflecting in his granny glasses. "Hey—," he says, "These Volt guys—they're going to make a mint. Just for writing checks and withholding taxes."

I scan the room, doing the mental math. About 300 contractors, with an average margin of maybe $10 per hour—whoa!—that's $3,000 per hour in gross profits, $24,000 per day, just for handling payroll and income tax reports. No wonder the Volt guys are licking their chops. Payroll . . . hmm . . . . How hard can that be? I could probably figure it out. And if I can't, Dad can. Yeah, I could work at Microsoft by day, and run a contracting firm by night.

I hoist my hand up, start waving. "Hey, Dick. Dick, I have a company." I rise. "I'll employ everyone." Dick's chilly blue eyes freeze. They're all looking at me: the scrappy contractors, the suits from Volt, Dick; they're all staring. They're all silent. Dick's eyes try to push me back into my seat, try to pull the air from my lungs. He's attempting to use the dark powers he thinks he has. I activate my deflector shield, an inside joke we engineers have, by pressing the right front belt loop on my jeans. Dan does the same, whispering, "Deflector shield activated!"

"Plus," I continue, "my firm takes a smaller cut of the employee's paycheck than Volt." My *firm*? *What* firm? As soon as this meeting ends I'll call 1-800-INCORPU and set one up. Volt's cut? Don't know how high it is, but I'm going to undercut it. In business that's called a *differentiator*. I read about it in *Inc.* magazine. I feel the folded magazine press against my back pocket, pushing me forward.

Turning, waiting, I gaze into the faces of the mostly male crowd. *C'mon,* I think. *Come with me. I have a better deal for you. C'mon.* Slowly, a few faces start to spark. They shine with the recognition that they are needed here, that they have a choice. "A chick boss?" "In what division?" The whispers start, and then amplify, multiply. "Software engineer or marketing babe? Better deal than Volt's?"

Dick twists his face, turns to me. "Well, that's an, uh, *interesting* proposal, Christine." He hates that I'm the first female contractor in the Operating Systems division. He hates that I have no degrees—not high school, not college. He hates me for tainting the Microsoft gene pool, the pool that was pristine and overflowing with Ivy League talent until I showed up. He hates that the contractors are considering me.

"Quiet down, everyone," Dick commands. No one hears him. The whispering has flared into talking, and 300 voices make a lot of noise, 300 voices generate a power that is palpable, so glaring you can feel the heat. "Everyone, everyone, listen up." The room is roaring. A tiny bead of sweat slides down Dick's crimson face. "Everyone, everyone . . . SHUT UP!" Dick shouts.

Affirmative, I think. *This guy is unstable biomatter.*

The two Volt guys are looking out at the crowd, shaking their heads, loosening their ties.

"So, everyone, go with Volt," Dick sputters.

I stand up, turn, and scan the crowd, making sure they see me. Me, their other option. Me, their Plan B.

"Oh, for Chrissakes," Dick says, his top lip curling, "or go with Christine's company. But become an employee within a week or you'll be *terminated*." He steps from the podium, straightens up, shakes hands with the suits from Volt. They glower at me, try to fry me with their thoughts. But they can't penetrate my deflector shield.

A small group of guys gather to hear my pitch. I stress that I'm an engineer and will undercut Volt by 5 percent. I hand out my e-mail address, t-chrisc@microsoft.com. Yes, I am a "t dash." Yes, I am temporary. But I'm here. I'm here now.

As everyone leaves the conference room I lag behind, looking for a phone. Ducking into an empty office, I slide the crumpled copy of *Inc.* magazine from my back pocket with tingly wet hands. *Dial. Dial the number.* What if I set up a company and no one wants to work for me? Or what if dozens do and I can't handle it? I still my trembling fingers. *Just dial. Dial the number.* Ten minutes and 100 bucks later, I have a Delaware corporation, Kuvera Associates. My mouth is tinny with the taste of fear.

Second call: an executive suite service. I need a temporary office. Like, now.

Third call: "Dad, payroll—how does it work?" He launches into a lengthy discourse on payroll taxes, the Employment Development Department (EDD), and the IRS. "Whoa!—what's the short version, Dad?"

"Tiger Baby, make it easy. Outsource to a payroll service. Let them handle it."

By the following morning I have e-mails from 35 contractors. Ohmygod. I meet with each prospective employee in my office rented by the hour. I wipe clammy hands on my new Ross Dress for Less pantsuit before the shake that seals each deal. By evening I have 35 employees.

I am in *way* over my head.

———————

When I first became a CEO I had no idea how to do it. I dove into business books and found out something superfast: to some extent, all first-time CEOs are making it up as they go along. This is what you do with a new job, a new role in life or business, a new community you are joining. You're declaring yourself to be something you aren't yet. You are intending it. You are *choosing* it. You're declaring victory as you step onto the battlefield. Then you're doing what it takes—applying the required skills and the hard work—to succeed in this new role.

Be a Quick-Change Artist

The best part about picking an illusion, which also could be called a self-image, is that you can change it if it doesn't work. Some illusions didn't empower me, so I moved on. Don't like what you see? Reinvent yourself!

The key is finding out what feeds your soul: which job, relationship, lifestyle, or type of community service.

The tricky part is when you've invested a lot in a given illusion and it's not working for you. Will you know when it's time to cut and run, to stop throwing good time and money after bad? Will you be honest enough to know whether it's time to move on or whether it's time to stay and stretch? Will you have the courage to follow through? Here's how to find out. Ask yourself the following questions:

- What does my current self-image "say" to others? What message does it project?

- Do I feel powerful and capable with my current self-image?

- If you're not satisfied with it, what's keeping you from changing? Complete this sentence: "If I could only [fill in the blank], I'd rule." Now go out and do what it takes to fill that blank in.

- Does my current self-image have untapped potential? Can I stretch/extend it to take me where I want to go?

An honest self-assessment based on answers to the questions above will help you determine if it's time to be a quick-change artist. One of my friends, Walter, is a talented and prolific writer. He often moans about the publishing industry, about how it feels closed to newcomers, how first-time authors have such a slim chance of getting published. I asked him how he saw the industry and his position in it. He said he sees the publishing industry as this enormous mansion, with manicured grounds. He's not even working in the garden—he's a farmhand way out on the South 40. The impressive entrance is barely visible from his distant field. As an indentured servant, he'll never even get *near* the publishing mansion.

I blurted out, "But everything's an illusion—so why not pick one that's empowering?" Walter asked how I, also new to the publishing scene, saw it. I said that to me the publishing world is a complex software system, and I am a talented hacker. Every day I make more progress navigating the system and getting closer to understanding how it works. It's a cool adventure, and I know I'll figure it out. Walter was silent for a moment, then said, "Wow. No wonder you have a terrific agent and a book deal." He took this to heart. Walter is changing his self-image and illusions of the publishing world, and I know one day soon he'll sell his first novel.

Sometimes you'll need to take several factors into consideration. You need to time your "quick change" in order to take into account money, family, and other factors. We need to be practical. Not everyone can move at an external speedy pace while still being responsible. I'm not advocating quitting your job before you've got your next gig lined up. I am, however, advocating quitting your destructive illusions—and pronto.

I came to a crossroads several years ago with a start-up where my cofounder and I had some serious disagreements. First, he wanted to be the chief executive

officer (CEO), a new position for him, and I reluc-
tantly agreed because he had deep knowledge of the industry we were targeting. I became the president and
chief technical officer (CTO). Then we had a clash over
both managerial style and treatment of people. I felt he
wanted to undercommunicate with our staff, telling
them the minimum they needed to know in order to
keep them in the dark so he'd have the upper hand. I
wanted to keep everyone in the loop, even overcommu-
nicate, while the team was in the formative stages. Bear
in mind that I had done the usual entrepreneurial
thing: worked without salary for a year, clocked 80-plus
hours a week, and made significant personal sacrifices.
I invested nothing short of my heart and soul. And still
it wasn't enough. The environment didn't work for me.
I couldn't fix what was broken, and the board wouldn't
help me either. A day came when I had to look in the
mirror and admit defeat. I had to bail on an illusion
that meant a lot to me: cofounder and CTO of this
particular start-up. Moving on was a wrenching decision, but it was the right one.

The good news is that I moved on and started another company. The better news is I kept in touch with
the company I'd left, offered help when asked, and ultimately was able to sell some of my stock to a new investor. It was a multimillion-dollar financial gain, and
yet I was able to respect myself by leaving a bad situation
and to respect the company by continuing to help out
from a healthy distance.

My greatest challenge when working with businesses

is getting them to change course after they've poured tremendous resources into making something happen that isn't working. *Remember: an illusion is something you use to change the reality around you. A delusion is something that prevents you from seeing the reality around you.* The companies that are suffering under delusions prefer to die a slow death by staying with a losing proposition rather than accepting the risk that comes with being a quick-change artist.

One company I worked with had invested 24 months and millions of dollars in developing its product strategy. I was called in because the product wasn't selling well and complaints about it were mounting. It was clear that they could attract more customers, and more quickly, by changing their product strategy. If they were to offer a more accessible, Web-based product, their customers would be less reliant on expensive consulting services. The company would attract more customers and have a faster, less expensive sales cycle.

The CEO, Tom, and I had a lively discussion that went nowhere. He had so much money, time, and ego invested in his original vision of the product plus how to sell it that he couldn't make a change, even after the board of directors recommended what I'd suggested. A new CEO, Henry, was brought in, but the story doesn't end there. Henry was so invested in his ideas about sales that he couldn't be a quick-change artist either. He spent time and money scaling up an expensive direct sales force, pushing the more accessible Web-based product onto the back burner. It was finally released about six months late, by which time the company was seriously short on cash. The company ended up being sold—to another "old-school" software company that was also late to the Web-based software party.

Fast-forward 12 months. Tom finally has a Web-based product—the very kind he'd protested against so vigorously—at his new company. Sales are going through the roof, and it's a belated happy ending—for him, at least. Henry is now working in obscurity at a huge company. Both CEOs could have spared themselves and their companies a lot of wasted energy and money if they'd been willing to let go of their ego investment in delusions that didn't work for them.

Sometimes you need to be a quick-change artist several times before you get it right; it takes courage and vision to change direction. One company I worked with started out as a consumer-focused business. After 12 long months of struggling to target a specific consumer niche with little success, they called me in. Together we decided that it would make more sense to focus on small businesses. The company had to rebrand itself with a new name, identity, and Web site, which required a huge outpouring of resources. Six months later, some of the company's biggest clients were large companies. They realized that the "small-business" client they were seeking was in reality a department within a large company. They tweaked their marketing message and homed in on work groups—whether in small, midrange, or big business. This final strategy worked; today their customers have virtual enterprise installations—built one work group at a time. This business made the transition and became successful and profitable because it was able to abandon its *delusion* of its target customer and serve its *real* one. The most successful executives are comfortable being quick-change artists; they have the vision and flexibility to let go of delusions and truly lead their teams.

Sometimes everything works too well. You're content, flourishing—but you're not growing or stretching, and you're possibly getting a little bored. You're ready for a new challenge; it's time to try a new illusion. For five years I wrote a column for the former Ziff Davis magazine, *PC Week*. I received hundreds of e-mails each month, keynoted countless conferences, and really felt that I was making a difference for my corporate readers who were struggling with rapid information technology adoption. But I knew I wasn't stretching any more. I'd settled into a too-comfortable groove, and I needed to let go and create space for something fresh to show up. So I asked myself the following questions:

- Can I see what the future will be like if I continue with this illusion?

- Do I feel excited and challenged by it?

- Would I have any long-term regrets by changing course now and designing and embracing a shiny new illusion?

With my answers (yep, nope, nope) I knew it was time to let go and leap. So I thanked my old illusion, which had taken me as far as it could, and transitioned out of my weekly column. That gave me the creative flexibility to look into myself for something that would help me grow, which turned out to be Artemis Ventures—a consultancy that did a little quick changing of its own and became a venture capital firm. There are two ways to approach life. One is to wake up each day and say, "I know what my life is going to be like today and that's what I want: predictability." The other is to say, "I have a rough idea of what my life is going to be like today and I can't wait to see what adventures show up! It's gonna be awesome!" I prefer the latter approach, which is why I love being a quick-change artist.

One of my friends, Diane Conway, author of *What Would You Do If You Had No Fear?*, challenges readers to describe their dream lives—and asks them to ponder the fears that are holding them back from realizing those dreams. Her current book is about what we'd do with our lives if we could start over. She and I did a reading a while back where she asked the audience, "How many of you would start over if you could?" I was stunned by the audience's response—about 80 percent of the people said they'd take the do over. I'm amazed at how many people lead lives of "quiet desperation," as Thoreau said. They're going through the motions, knowing that what they're doing isn't working, but they're too stuck, comfortable, or scared to change it. These are exactly the kinds of people who need to be reminded that everything is an illusion. It's never too late to pick an illusion that's more empowering.

If a new illusion doesn't work, don't get mad; get material. Your past is useful. Look at it, but don't stare. All experience is good. Ask yourself the above questions about changing illusions and design another one. Then make it come true. And always remember that if you don't select an illusion, a self-identity, someone will select one for you. Wouldn't you rather be the decision maker?

Evicting the Vile Bitch

So what's stopping you? Well, if you're like most of us, fear raises its ugly head just when the fun starts. But here's the good news: your fears are only illusions. Some fear is good. Fear that is survival oriented is essential. Fear that is motivating helps us keep going on the tough days. But mostly our fears are just a kind of illusion, and not even a special kind. When I work with entrepreneurs and intrapreneurs, I find we share a lot of common fears.

So, how can you banish them? Since fear is mostly about ignorance, the best part is that it's as temporary as you choose. I used to make "fear lists" and tackle one a month, reviewing the lists at least twice a year to see if I'd successfully banished the demons. Now I just tackle my fears in real time, as they come up. Some of my past fears included attending events where I felt inadequate (not important enough) and ignorant about socializing with superpowerful people. My palms would get ice cold and clammy, and my posture would be "small" and a little hunched. It was clear I didn't feel in their league. I wanted to play at this level of business and society but was scared.

Shortly after I decided to nail this fear, one of my mentors invited me to a dinner party in New York. I was seated at a table with Connie Chung, Maury Povich, and several other famous and powerful people. I had to shake a ton of hands and make small talk for 90 minutes when I had no idea what these people were interested in. I adopted an illusion that I too was a player, powerful and famous, and willed my palms to be dry and warm. I asked a lot of questions. I was confident. And the result was that now I can meet anyone, speak before any size crowd, and hold my own.

Identify that inner critic, that fearmonger, inside your head. Draw a picture of her or him and write down what she or he says. Mine is quite the blabbermouth: *Stop making so many mistakes! You're fat, work out more! You're not making a big enough contribution to the world—work harder, do more, give more! You're a fraud—you're not as smart or accomplished as you think you are!* Maybe your inner critic is a schoolmarm, an icky blob monster, or a dominatrix. Name yours, if you want. My friend, comedienne Terri Tate, calls hers "That Vile Bitch Upstairs." Then when you hear her shrieking, say, "Thanks for sharing. Please take a: vacation/chill pill/nap."

What are you afraid of? Why? Are you afraid you won't be liked? Get over it. Renegades rarely win popularity contests. It's not a choice: you have a passion you're pursuing because you have to, not because it's going to make people like you. Female executives seem to struggle the most with this, because some of us are told that ambition is bad. If this resonates with you, read Debra Condren's book *AmBITCHous* to get clarity on this misconception. I worked with one woman who deeply believed that leadership was about getting the consensus of her team. It's not. Leadership is about listening to your team, and then making decisions on your own. This exec was so desperate to be liked by her team that she dithered over the simplest decision, hoping against hope that she would get unanimous approval. The result? Countless missed opportunities, products late to market—appearing behind those of even the slowest competitors—and a company that's what I call "living dead."

Are you afraid your emotions will get in the way of your success? Jealousy's a big one. I've fallen prey to this energy zapper personally and professionally. *Jealousy and envy are often about comparing our insides to someone else's outsides—a symptom of our externally focused world.* But how can you really know what it's like to be someone else? Maybe inside they don't have such a great life after all. You'll probably never know, and I've been amused to discover how many times I've been flat-out wrong about someone else's situation. The tabloids are all about this: people devour gossip about celebrities and their "ideal" relationships, only to find they've been living in misery and are divorcing months after their "happy couple" photos were plastered all over the newsstands. The net-net is that they have *their* life. Let them. Focus on living *your* life. As Jack Canfield told me, you're the composite of the five people you spend the most time with. Are the dominant people in your life positive and uplifting? Or negative and draining? (Or are *you* negative and draining? Introspection is not synonymous with whining.) Assess and make your choices wisely. Your energy is precious; spend it only where you want to.

Afraid that there's only so much of "it" out there, and you have no chance to get it? No way; that's just another illusion. Scarcity is a lie. There's plenty for everyone. Every day the Department of the Treasury is printing more money, the sun is generating more energy, new people are coming into your life, new opportunities are being created. That's how the world works: everything is in motion. Atoms teach us this. Equilibrium is a dynamic state.

Think you need to be more like someone else to succeed? Forget it. The second you start thinking that way, you'll become a counterfeit version of both yourself and your model, and believe me, that won't make you a success. Learn from other people, people you know and people you read about, but make what you learn your own.

Afraid you'll fail? That's a big one, big enough for its own chapter. But don't worry—there's no such thing as failure. We'll dive into this in Chapter 5.

Until you've learned to ignore your inner critic, your fears will feel like reality, not illusion. Anyone can fall into this trap. I have a friend who's a communications coach. A dynamic, intelligent, single woman, she really wants to be in a relationship. But she told me that while she's dressing to go out, she'll look in the mirror and say, "I'm old, I'm fat, no one's going to want to talk to me, I'm not going to this party." Years ago, I had a friend who was five feet tall and a size 14. She was a regular gal, no high-powered job, no major advantages in life. Every day while she was getting dressed, she'd look in the mirror and say to herself, "Honey, how could you get more gorgeous? I just don't know!" She'd date the most stunning guys right out of a *GQ* spread! She was attracting guys that matched the way she envisioned herself: HOT.

Meanwhile I was attracting guys who matched what I thought I deserved: bad boys who didn't treat me with respect. That only changed when I remembered it's all an illusion. So I picked an illusion that's empowering and started meeting smart, nice, cool guys. Recruit a trusted friend to be your sounding board, both for your self-image and for your body language. You need to be aware of the nonverbal messages you are sending to the world, because people are definitely reacting to them. I often get all sorts of crazy favors, such as fabulous hotel room upgrades and reservations at fully booked restaurants because my body language and tone of voice convey that I am worthy of these perks. I don't convey a vibe of entitlement, which can put people off; it's more of a "surely we can work something out together" vibe that includes the other person in the inner sanctum that I want access to. If you're speaking professionally, hire a coach to check out your body language. Learn to stand and speak in a way that conveys: I'm here, I have value, I'm holding the floor.

A phrase I've heard a lot is "fake it till you make it." Believe me, I know the fear that phrase is born from. Imagining yourself into a different place doesn't mean you should be a fake or act fraudulently. It isn't about faking out others: it's about faking out the vile bitch exercising squatter's rights over your psyche. Once you realize that just about everyone is making it up as they go along, it gets a lot easier.

I prefer *"Act it until you ARE it."* Act as if you know how to be a CEO, act as if you've already received the promotion when you pitch your boss for it; it'll help you transcend the fear and self-doubt inherent in taking a career leap. Act as if your company is substantial and important when pitching your product to a key executive of a huge multinational company; you'll transmit your confidence and belief in your business.

Yes, I still have some self-doubt. Yes, I still obsess sometimes. But neither of these fear-driven behaviors has the power to sabotage me anymore. With the tools described in this chapter, I've learned to banish many of my fears and manage the few that persist. I've learned that sometimes my strongest supporters will be baffled when I try on a new illusion, because I "sold" them so well on my previous one. But the only true opposition is the evil bitch upstairs. When she offers me unwelcome judgments or advice, I remind myself, "Heck, it's all an illusion."

CHRISTINE'S QUICK 'N' EASY WAY TO SET AND ACHIEVE GOALS

Goal setting is the best way to build your dreams and reinforce a new self-identity. Desire comes first; you've got to want something badly. Then goals become the way you'll manifest your desires. Set *specific* goals based on your desires, see and feel them happening. Put yourself in that glorious future in your mind. Then *get out of the way*. There's no room for doubt or self-sabotage here. To quote Einstein, "Imagination is everything—it is the preview of life's coming attractions."

- Set one to three goals in each of these seven categories: Financial/Wealth, Career/Business, Free Time/Fun, Health/Appearance, Relationships, Personal Development/Learning, Community/Charity. If this feels too overwhelming, just pick your top three goals and focus on those. In time you'll be ready to add more. This isn't homework—it should be fun! You're shaping your future and bringing what you want into your life. How cool to know that this is something you can effect!

- Write one goal per index card. Write in the present tense, starting with "I am" and using an active verb. Give it a due date, and then be sure to append "or sooner" to the end as well as "or more" or "or less" to amounts. Example: "I am enjoying weighing 125 or less

(continues)

by September 30, 2007 or sooner," or "I am celebrating $10 million or more in revenue for my company by December 31, 2008 or sooner." Now you have your goal deck of seven to 21 cards.

- Go through the goal deck at least twice a day. Visualize achieving your goals, experiencing the good feelings associated with your success. After reviewing your deck in the morning, write down three things you can do today to help achieve your number 1 goal. Also write down any ideas that float up while you're visualizing your success; you'll act on them later.

- Create a "dream board" as described in Chapter 2 of pictures you draw or clip from magazines illustrating what you want to achieve, to become, or to get.

- Mark time out on your calendar for growth and personal development. I go to two or more self-improvement seminars per year, in addition to solo retreats. You'll return to your life, work, relationships, and service with new insights and renewed energy.

- Remember that focusing on your goals isn't enough. You need to keep your ears and eyes open for opportunities and do the work required to achieve these goals.

If you need more help blasting through negative illusions, here are two fantastic resources. Read *Ten Days* to *Self-Esteem* by Dr. David Burns, and actually *do* the exercises—I got more from this workbook than I did from over $3,000 in therapy—and all for $15! I also recommend Jack Canfield's *Breakthrough to Success* training. This intense week-long seminar will change your life. You'll leave feeling lighter, more present, more in touch with who you are.

COOL FREE RESOURCES

Go to www.RulesForRenegades.com and download "Goal Setting Worksheet," "New Illusion Worksheet," and "Future Planning Worksheet," and see the Personal Development section, too.

2

An MBA Is Optional, a GSD Is Essential

Kissing the Blarney Stone and Then Some Butt

Ideas are a dime a dozen. People who implement them are priceless.

MARY KAY ASH

YOU WEREN'T BORN into a life of privilege? Didn't go to the right college? Don't have a trust fund? Welcome to the meritocracy of entrepreneurship: *results* are what bestow privilege, create credentials, and build bucks. People think there's a secret sauce to success that comes with social class, family, or knowing which fork to use. Nope. Hey, connections help a ton, but you can make them on your own. You don't need Daddy's. What matters is getting your foot in the door and then delivering quality results—consistently and on time.

Being successful has little to do with collecting the right pieces of paper from the right college. I'm not knocking the benefit of a good education, but I'm more interested in your GSD: your Gets Stuff Done. Real-world results are what counts, not the pile of degrees you acquire or the pretend-world case studies you pore over. That said, education builds your skill set and boosts your credibility. Degrees can open doors, too. With a high school diploma, my career path would've had fewer potholes, It may have even been relatively smooth if I had a college degree. My concern is that you add the key credential of a GSD to your existing set of skills. True, some people may need certain degrees to get a particular job. But real-world results will help you climb the corporate ladder faster and with greater fulfillment.

Fast-Forward for Fun and Fulfillment

If you feel you have enough background and enough maturity to fast-forward into the next phase of your life, go for it. It's important to let those feelings take over and start to make things happen. Don't stick with the status quo just because it's comfortable or familiar—that's what society tells us to do. It took me a while to learn that just because something is expected of you doesn't mean you have to do it. Take high school, for instance. At mine, senior year was a total bust. Everyone just partied and went to football games. So I decided to skip it. Patience isn't always a virtue.

I talked my way into the University of California, San Diego so I could leave high school at the end of my junior year. After a couple of years in the major-of-the-month club, it seemed that getting some work experience was a better idea. I dropped out of college, moved to Los Angeles, and found a job as a receptionist at a start-up private bank. Bingo! I loved business. It was fun, fulfilling, and focusing. Within four months I was signing up new accounts, and in two more I was in charge of the vault—and about $2 million in cash. A pager clipped to my waist kept me available to customers 24/7. The only downside was the career path—I'd already gotten as far as I could go without a college degree, so at age 20 I gave college one last try, this time at UCLA. Majoring in English, I found a part-time job doing research on an Apple IIe computer. I liked computers. They weren't inconsistent or confusing, as I often found people to be. Being a programmer meant mobility, flexibility, and limited human interaction. Perfect. But a computer science major would mean three more years in school, so I embraced my inner geek and taught myself how to program PCs. I left UCLA without a degree and worked a few programming jobs. Finally, I accepted my impatience, my need to forge my own path. After a couple of years, I decided I was ready for the big time: a job at Microsoft. Here's how it went down:

――――――――――

The guys from Microsoft come to Houlihan's every Wednesday night, where I moonlight waiting tables for extra cash. Bill Gates has vowed to make Windows the world standard, and Windows programming experience is hard to find, so if I have some, the guys say I should go for it and submit my résumé. Luckily, one of the guys, Tony, has given me some work writing code for his company on the side, and Greg has agreed to vouch for me as a friend of Tony's. But neither can get me into Microsoft: I have to figure that out on my own.

Just a few teensy problems. I don't have the requisite engineering degree—hell, I don't have any degree. And let's face it—I'm a chick, which doesn't improve my odds in the world of 1980s engineering. But I know I have the skills, attitude, and drive for this job. No sheepskin, but definitely a degree—a

GSD—in my hip pocket, plus a pile of letters of recommendation from previous bosses. I'm taking a three-pronged approach to increase my chances: (1) enter through the back door as a temp worker through a contracting firm, (2) enter through the front door, applying for a permanent post to Microsoft Human Resources, (3) enter through the side door by calling the head of Windows engineering and giving him my opinion of the many ways in which Windows sucks. He'll at least have to respond to me with an approach like that.

I've sent my résumé to the contracting firm; now I need to apply to HR and then call the head of Windows. Hunched over my kitchen table, I'm filling out the job application when I stop at the box marked "Gender." There are only two choices. If I pick the first, "Male," I'm likely to be offered an interview; once I get my foot in the door, I'll just have to talk fast and sell myself well. I might even land a job. If I check the second box, "Female," chances are excellent that there'll be no interview and no offer. No thanks. I can't let them blow me off before they meet me. I've got to get my foot in the door.

The future is in Windows and I'll be part of it, whatever it takes. I've come too far to turn back now. I check the "Male" box and attach my résumé, name edited from Christine to Chris. I'm kind of scared, because in addition to the gender issue I've left the education section intentionally vague. I give the dates when I was in high school and college and the degree I was working on. It'll be okay unless they look carefully, count the years. Then they'll figure it out: no high school diploma, no college degree. If they ask, will I tell? Fingering my worn sandalwood prayer beads I think, *Please. Please help me get a job at Microsoft.*

Three days later the phone rings. "Hi, is Chris there? This is Marie from Microsoft Human Resources."

"Oh, gosh, Chris isn't here. May I take a detailed message? Chris likes lots of details in messages."

"Okay, please let him know we've scheduled an interview with the Applications Division next Thursday at one o'clock. I'd appreciate a call to confirm."

"You know, Marie, just this morning Chris said next Thursday's wide open. Why don't I just confirm now on Chris's behalf? Chris will be there. Thanks so much for calling. Have a nice day." Get her off the phone, don't let her second-guess you.

"Um, okay, uh, thanks." Hesitating, Marie hangs up.

Phew! Okay, all I have to do is become male in five days. One interview booked, two to go. Now I've got to call the Operating Systems division. If I can land an interview before next Thursday, I can say another division is already in hot pursuit of me. Microsoft is infamous for battles over talent among divisions. There's only one way to land an interview with the head of Windows: cold calling.

A few weeks ago I read an article in *PC Magazine* about Windows. I saved it for the name of the guy interviewed. He didn't have great verbal skills and had come across as a snotty engineer. Good. If I can just get him on the phone, then perhaps I can talk my way into an interview. If I can get an interview, I'll figure out how to avoid being kicked out of his office when I ask for a job. I dial the main Microsoft number and ask for Ryan. Time to remember to "*Act* it until you *ARE* it."

"Hi, Ryan. I just thought I'd let you know that Microsoft Windows is a great idea." My voice is low, neutral. Hmm . . .

hope I sound like a guy—or at least not too much like a girl. I can't let him hang up on me.

"Well, thanks. We take pride in using superior software engineering techniques, and we believe Windows will be the PC desktop standard shortly."

Shortly? Hello? Windows has a handful of test installations worldwide, and none are being used by nontechnical people. Yeah, it'll be a worldwide standard tomorrow. Is this guy deluded or what? "There's just one little problem," I venture.

"Uh, and what's that?"

"It's really hard to use. I mean, it's a great idea, but a lame design."

"Well, if you're so smart, why don't you come fix it?" I can practically see the sneer on Ryan's face.

"Terrific. I'll be there in an hour. I'll call you from the lobby. Oh, by the way, my name is Chris Comaford. Bye." Click. Pacing across the brown shag carpet of my tiny apartment, I have to face it: I have no plan. I'm just going to walk in, stun the guy with my brilliant ideas, and then count on a miracle happening. I'm as ready as I'll ever be. I nerve myself up by reviewing my strong points: my Windows programming abilities, my unbiased design opinions, my massive perseverance, and the people I know.

After schmoozing the receptionist, I have the lowdown on Ryan. (You've got to learn all you can about your intended target.) I call him from the Building Three lobby phone. He appears pronto. "You're . . . you're . . . a chick!" Stammering, his eyes bug out. "Whoa, I didn't actually expect you to show up. . . . I mean, I didn't really take you seriously." He turns his body at an angle to me, leaning his head back suspiciously, a private eye peeping from under his fedora.

Geez, who is this guy? "Yes, Ryan, I am a chick. Regardless, I actually do know how to code, in Assembly, COBOL, RPG, a little FORTRAN, C, and the Windows 1.03 APIs." My arms hang at my sides, I hold my head high. This is my Confident Stance. I always apply it in tricky situations. Whether I feel confident or not, I think of something I know a lot about, and project that power, that certainty.

"No way." He is backing up now, as if preparing to turn and walk away.

"Yes, way. Want me to solve some coding problems? I can make Windows crash, and then disassemble the code to show you where some of the bugs are." I wink and walk toward him.

He takes another step back, and I push onward—you're not getting away this easily, Mister.

Squinting his eyes, still leaning his head back, "Yeah?"

"Yeah, Ryan. So, shall we have a conversation in your office? Windows can be a PC desktop standard with a few little enhancements. Let's go." I guide him down the hall to the row of offices. Sure, this guy is kinda creepy, but I want a job here. I won't be blown off by some sexist dweeb.

Our "chat"—clearly that's what Ryan thinks it is—is going pretty well. I, however, am determined to get him to see this as an interview. I tell him the obvious stuff, that Windows should mimic a real physical desktop with overlapping documents and files. Not a new idea, true, but maybe a chick hasn't said it.

"So, Ryan, I know a lot of secretaries, and for secretaries to use Windows, we'll have to increase their efficiency. If Windows can do that, it will spread throughout corporate America and eventually dominate the world." Ryan is looking around the office, barely listening, as if terribly bored. Only when he hears "dominate the world" do his ears prick up, a hunting dog hearing the bugle. TWD, or Total World Domination, is the favorite three-letter acronym at Microsoft. Another thing I learned in my due diligence.

"Yeah, I hear a lot about overlapping Windows, but I think we need to stick with tiled Windows. People will get lost navigating. The windows in our environment will remain tiled side by side." *No one can work in little tiled windows. Constantly resizing them is a major pain in the butt. This technique will never take off with busy secretaries—or anyone else, for that matter.* Ryan stands up and tips his head toward the door. "Well, it's been interesting talking with you. Bye."

Time's running out. Better resort to shameless name dropping. "Ryan, I can help here, and I know a bunch of guys that agree. Tony in Systems and Greg in Applications think I'd make a terrific addition to the Windows team."

"You know Tony and Greg? They're *gods.*" Ryan's eyes open wide, and he looks at me—not through me—for the first time. "Well, I'll call them and see what they say about you. We have some slots for testers coming open," he says, scoffing at me.

Offering a programmer a testing position is highly insulting. It's like putting a five-star chef on the line at Denny's. Ryan's still stuck on the "chicks can't code" crap. I refuse to register the slap. My Confident Stance is incompatible with insults. "Actually, I was thinking of a programmer position. HR has booked me an interview next week with the Applications division." I face him dead-on, standing my ground.

"Yeah, I'll think about it, whatever," turning his back on me, he sits at his desk and begins working. Meeting over. I feel great that I didn't get psyched out or thrown out. But I still doubt Ryan will give me a job. What else can I try?

The next day I am summoned to Microsoft—and not by Ryan. So what? Getting your foot in the door requires keeping one's options open. The contracting firm I'd pitched (my "backdoor" option) had come through. One grueling 10-hour day later, after interviewing with eight different programmers, writing countless lines of code, identifying and fixing too many bugs to remember, and answering absurd story problems, I'm sent home to collapse.

———————————

"Chris" never interviewed with Marie in HR, thank God. I wasn't planning on dressing in drag, but would have, if I had to. "Christine" got a job as a tester, which I initially found ego squashing but decided was a foot in the door. I eventually moved into programming, but I had to work at a competitor, Lotus, in that role first.

Sometimes you have to go in the back or side door. So what? As long as you come out the front. I knew I had the goods, and I figured that with three different approaches, one of them would have to fly. That's the beauty of having your GSD.

Ow! That's My Foot in There!

More often than not, earning a GSD requires getting your foot in the door. My friend Charles was dying to speak at a high-profile conference. Getting this gig would "make" his career: he'd gain massive credibility, sell tons of products, and essentially get an instant customer base. I introduced him via e-mail to the woman in charge of the conference, and Charles proceeded to call and e-mail her over the course of four months. She replied to the first e-mail and then went radio silent. He was thoroughly frustrated because he knew he'd do a great job but couldn't get the decision maker to communicate. He asked me what to do. "Charles, we both know she'll be in L.A. next week at one of her events. Get in the car, drive down to the hotel, and make it a point to meet her. It can't be that hard! Go for it!" Charles juggled his schedule, schlepped four hours (round-trip) for a 10-minute meeting with the conference organizer, and inked the deal. He earned his GSD that day, and his career has hit warp speed.

As an intrapreneur you'll need your GSD too, and often it involves acting like an owner of the business. Harold, a procurement manager at a manufacturing company, wanted real-time quotes from suppliers in order to reduce costs, avoid overpaying, and improve operational efficiency. He repeatedly cost-justified the company's need for this system, and eventually management considered it by hiring a pricey consulting firm to do a four-month assessment! Harold was mortified—four months to render an opinion? He convinced his boss to let him do an experiment, which would require a few hours a day from his team for a few weeks. The initial progress was so positive that his boss gave him more time, and in three months his team had built a real-time quote system. Management realized their error, increased their faith in the expertise of their staff, and let the consultants go. GSDs in hand, Harold's team has saved the company over $300 million to date.

Often earning a GSD requires listening to that quiet voice inside. About 18 months ago, I felt it was urgent that I call Veronica, a prospect I'd been chasing for six months. I dialed her number, but when her voice mail kicked in I had a moment of doubt. Had my intuition failed me? Then she picked up the phone, mid—voice mail. I repeated my pitch again, and she said she'd just told her staff about me. A deal with her firm was a goal I had focused on twice daily for eight months. The deal we did involved my delivering a seminar at one of her events. I met a few hundred budding entrepreneurs there, and am now helping several dozen of them accelerate their businesses via mentoring calls and our CD series for start-ups.

Getting a GSD also requires goal setting, which helps you both clarify your purpose in your career and plan your next two promotions. You may not be able to visualize yourself as the CEO, but what are the next two rungs you want to climb? What will it take to get there? Do the grunt work others aren't willing to do. You may not always get credit for what you do; just remember, you're out to make your name—and your "brand" (more on this in Chapter 4) synonymous with results. Ask specifically for more opportunity; this means more work but also more recognition. Treat your personal development like the development of a business—you need to be well rounded and have all "departments" thrive. Fun, personal growth, service, and relationships are just as important as finance, career, and health. How will you make your life a profitable, well-run company?

Vampires and Other Vexations

Let's talk about toxic people. They come in many shapes and forms. I've worked with several people who've told me I wouldn't understand something, not to "worry my pretty head about it," implying the issue was too complex for me to grasp. In the beginning I fell for this. Later I'd realize I missed out on a cool opportunity because someone had psyched me out. This flavor of toxicity can be particularly lethal because it can come in the guise of protectiveness or helpfulness, but the real result is to make you feel incompetent or insufficient. Another type of psych-out is information withholding. This is when a coworker doesn't tell you things that are important to succeed at your job—until it's too late. For a crash course on psych-outs, see the movie *BASEketball* from the creators of *South Park*. The main thrust of the movie is how a sports team psychs out its competition via personal insults and mind games.

Even friends can be deflators. I've had some who'd run an endless tape loop about the same old complaints, over and over. I'd be emotionally drained after each call or visit. Eventually it struck me that they weren't doing anything to improve their lives; for whatever reason, they wanted a lousy life. I knew I needed friends who shared my desire to be positive and progressive, so it was time to change the situation or say goodbye. In this case there are two things you can do. First, list all of the toxic person's *positive* qualities. Hold these qualities in mind when you think of him or her. The toxic person might start to shift to become more positive since you are no longer reinforcing his or her negativity. (You can also use this process with your own fears or bad habits.) If this doesn't work, then you'll likely need to let go.

When you have to let go of destructive relationships, do it with compassion. Tell the person that he or she is a fine human being; your life is simply going in a different direction. You need to surround yourself with people who share your goals for self-improvement. But what if you can't? What if the toxic person is your boss, a coworker, a family member? Try the "Three E's" in Chapter 7. Spend as little time around that person as possible, use your Confident Stance, remember your deflector shield, conveniently activated from your pants belt loop! Feel compassion for the pain the individual must be in. Why else would he intentionally try to hurt others or bring them down with his bad attitude? Visualize all his negativity bouncing off of you. Consider that it might be time to find a more positive work environment. You'll notice that the more engaged you are in designing your ideal work environment and life, the less often toxic people will want to be around you. Your positive energy will turn them off.

Let's Get Visual

When I was an hourly contractor at Microsoft, I hung a poster in my cubicle entitled "My First Million." It showed a pile of cash—$1 million. I focused on it daily, knowing I'd hatch that million-dollar idea. I made my first million within two years of buying the poster and yes, after doing the required work. I did a similar visualization a few years ago when seeking my dream home. I cut out a picture of a gorgeous view of vineyards, and yes, within a year I'd found a house with that exact view at a reasonable price. I've had photos of girlfriends hanging out to bring more girl time into my life and photos of couples cuddling to bring more intimacy into my marriage.

Make a "dream board" of the pictures that speak to you. They will help you affirm your intention and mobilize your energies toward achieving your goals. Yes, this stuff really works! Remember Veronica? Had I not listened to that voice inside that said "Call Veronica *now*," I could have chased her for another six months. When you achieve one of these goals, write it down—this will keep your energy mobilized and will remind you that you're making progress on the tough days. I want to be clear here. I'm not talking about some magical process where the universe sprinkles fairy dust on you because you think pretty thoughts. I'm talking about the power you mobilize within yourself, consciously and subconsciously, when you make the effort to clarify your goals and visualize them as being achieved, while doing the required legwork.

Frequent Flying with the Fab Four

The key to your GSD is to avoid being overly pushy, which turns people off and makes them back away from helping you. I'll admit that it's been a lifelong challenge for me to learn when to back off if I'm coming on too strong and to appreciate that other people sometimes enjoy a stroll instead of a sprint. I rein myself in by frequently using the four most important phrases in business and life:

- "Please"
- "Thank you"
- "I'm sorry"
- "I don't know"

I can't tell you how often I've decided against hiring someone, agreeing to be a mentor, or taking on a client because he or she can't say these four simple things. The first two require basic manners. When you say "please" you're reminding yourself and acknowledging to others that nobody owes you anything and their help to you is a gift. When you say, "thank you" you're taking the time to acknowledge that effort and gift. Both phrases require a quality of awareness that transcends simple manners. They're the essence of good business and good living.

The third phrase in the Fab Four requires humility and guts. Why is it so hard for us to say we're sorry when we mess up? You'll make mistakes, so cop to them and clean them up. A true apology not only acknowledges your mistake; it includes an implicit promise to make amends for what you did wrong. Beware—an apology in no way obligates the other party to apologize for her share of wrongdoing. If that happens, terrific, but it has nothing to do with your desire to apologize. If you're not sure how to make amends for what you've done wrong, just say: "I'm sorry. I screwed up. How can I make it up to you?" The loss of time or money is worth the goodwill your effort will engender and the ongoing business relationship it will support. Studies show that doctors are far less likely to get slapped with malpractice suits when they tell their patients up front what they feel they have done wrong or could have done better.

A while back I sat on the board of a start-up with a CEO, Rianne, who was brilliant—but who couldn't stop overselling. She was brought in to turn around a failing company, and within two years she had repositioned the product line and boosted sales to $9 million, which was no mean feat. Rianne's Achilles' heel was that she loved to pump up the team with stories about their glorious future, even when that future was unlikely to materialize. She'd tell everyone at the staff meeting about the big deals in process, and how they would close imminently. She told the board the same stories. The trouble was, the deals frequently didn't happen.

Ultimately, Rianne's key executives began calling the board members in an attempt to get the truth. But we were being snowed too. She began to lose credibility, which was bad, but even worse, she couldn't bring herself to say, "I'm sorry, I shouldn't have spoken about all these deals until they were done." Instead she danced around the issue or defended herself.

Our trust in Rianne was destroyed, and we had to let her go. The company almost tanked. Today it's struggling to achieve $3 million in sales. Had she followed our advice to keep her rosy projections in check and apologize for her loose lips, she'd still be in charge and the company would be thriving, not barely surviving. Would I hire her again? Yes, if she'd avoid the same mistake and had learned the Fab Four.

It can be just as hard for many of us to admit what we don't know. We feel weak, stupid, vulnerable. It's tough to stand in front of people, be they staff members or stockholders—especially if they're the angry, pitchfork-wielding type—and say you don't know something. It feels lousy. Let it. It'll pass.

You won't know everything, so let the people around you know that and tell them when you'll find the answer. They won't hold it against you: they'll actually admire your courage instead. Stand up and say, "I don't know the answer to that, but it's a good question. I'll find out and get back to you in a few days." Then tell them how you'll find the answer, and ask if they have any suggestions. This will make them part of the solution, and they'll likely want you to succeed. Then honor your commitment—because they're watching and will notice if you don't get back to them!

Similarly, when someone has the courage to tell you that he or she doesn't know something, affirm that the person is doing the right thing in admitting it. I can't stand it when I admit I'm ignorant about something only to hear, "You don't know?" in a voice full of incredulity. This kind of reaction closes down honest communication. And once that door has been slammed, it takes a long time to pry it open again. Regaining trust can be a lengthy process.

Todd, a first-time CEO I worked with was a brilliant, sophisticated financial executive. Formerly a CFO at a successful start-up that had had a glorious initial public offering (IPO), he was well versed in how to interact with the board of directors. Todd didn't have a strong sales and marketing background, but that wouldn't have been a big deal if he had recruited a vice president of sales who could have filled in this blank spot in his résumé. Unfortunately, he couldn't bring himself to say "I don't know." Todd was so accustomed to knowing it all as CFO that he refused to have a beginner's mind. So when trouble appeared (as it often does), he wouldn't ask for sales and marketing advice. We offered it, repeatedly, but often he wouldn't take it, since that would have been an admission of his blind spot. Alas, we had to let Todd go.

Once you have your GSD in your hip pocket, you'll have one of the most valuable "credentials" a person can possess. You'll understand what you're good at, and this understanding will expand as you continue to grow your skill set and stretch into unfamiliar areas. You'll be able to identify other holders of GSDs and have the chance to work with them. Whether as a team leader or a team member, your GSD puts you into the steeplechase. Go!

TEN STEPS TO YOUR GSD

A GSD means always maximizing your forward motion while minimizing your drag coefficient. Here are 10 steps to build your momentum.

1. *Rock responsibility.* Say bye-bye to blaming others because your life isn't working or you don't have what you want. Ditto for complaining, which is blame disguised. You're no one's victim. Everything in our lives, good or bad, is the result of our actions or thoughts. When we take 100 percent responsibility for our lives we're acknowledging this, which then enables us to improve our situation. Responsibility is an active pursuit. What would happen if you took just 5 percent more responsibility in your life? You'll be amazed by the results!

2. *Get visual.* In Chapter 1, I gave you detailed tips on and techniques for setting goals. They're important and deserve a long look, since you'll want to set specific goals, visualize them being achieved, and act on making them happen. Your goals should include what specifically you want to achieve and when specifically you want to achieve them. For instance, you could create a promotion plan and ask your boss if you achieve X, Y, Z goals would that warrant a promotion and pay raise of ___ percent? Keep track of how you're progressing. It will work wonders in focusing yourself and keeping you on track.

3. *Solicit superb support.* A supportive tribe is necessary to a GSD. I've found two hugely effective ways to do that: an accountability partner and a mastermind group. An accountability partner is a friend or colleague who will help you stay accountable to your commitments. A mastermind group is a group of like-minded people who help further one another's goals on a group basis. See the resources at the end of this chapter for info on how to establish accountability partners and mastermind groups.

4. *Toss toxicity.* You probably have some toxic people in your life right now. They're the folks who seem to want to hold you back or bring you down. Know anyone who actively hampers your ability to advance? Creates fires you have to waste time stamping out? Tells you that you can't do what you're doing? They're deflators—Dr. Judith Orloff calls them "energy vampires." You can choose to avoid them or let their negativity bounce off of you. If you're not sure if someone is toxic, just monitor how you feel after spending time with that person. Feel furious? Exhausted? Despondent? You've got a live one: get out the isolation suit!

5. *Pump up the positive.* Use only positives when you talk to yourself about your goals. Negative self-talk fosters a negative self-image, which results in negative behaviors. We sabotage ourselves far more than anyone sabotages us. ("See? I knew they wouldn't hire

(continues)

me/ask me out/give me the sales award.") List your strengths. Don't list your shortcomings; instead, reframe them as strengths you want to develop. Be honest if you have no interest in improving in a certain area and be okay with it. I, for instance, have zero desire to become a terrific organizer. So I hire someone who is. Another way to accentuate the positive is to read and reread inspiring books. Listen to uplifting, motivating CDs or podcasts. Surround yourself with upbeat energy.

6. *Log on to the Law of Attraction.* You won't find it in Newtonian physics, but I live by a very cool rule in the universe called the Law of Attraction. You've heard the saying "What you focus on, you become." That's the idea of the Law of Attraction. When you develop a clear idea of what you want, focus on it, and feel good about it, your mind will consider your wishes to be marching orders. The universe will conspire to help to make your dreams come true. This is why you have to know what you want, look at images of what you want, imagine yourself already having it, and do the work required to make your dreams come true. As Norman Vincent Peale put it, "Formulate and stamp indelibly on your mind a mental picture of yourself as succeeding. Hold this picture tenaciously. Never permit it to fade. Your mind will seek to develop the picture."

7. *Persevere.* As I'll discuss more thoroughly in Chapter 5, you're probably going to have a healthy number of so-called failures and rejections in your career and life. The key is how you view them and whether you let them hold you back. I think of failures as "learning adventures" to reduce their negative impact. As Henry Ford said, "Failure gives us the opportunity to begin again more intelligently." It's okay to be afraid, and it's certainly okay to fail, and everybody gets rejected. Prepare for these inevitable knocks. Hang Mother Teresa's *Do It Anyway* (which appears in this book's Conclusion) in your office at eye level. Read it often, especially on challenging days.

8. *Pay attention.* One of the fundamental attitudes you need to cultivate is constantly paying attention to what's going on around you, as I discuss in Chapter 3. That may seem obvious, but it's not just about focusing closely on what you're doing. Sometimes when you're concentrating on what you're doing, you miss the important stuff. While you're concentrating on the cracks in the sidewalk, you miss the rainbow. We all are oblivious at times, but the more you increase your attention to life, the more present you are, the more you'll notice opportunities. Cultivate the ability to laser focus *and* scan your surroundings.

9. *Continuously course-correct.* We all make mistakes. I'll talk about this more in Chapter 7, but the big idea

(continues)

is that the more honest we are, the more likely we'll avoid mistakes or recognize them immediately and be able to clean them up quickly. The more we clean up our messes, the less guilt, regret, or baggage we have, the lighter our load is (reducing our drag coefficient), and the easier it becomes to rise above petty issues and see more clearly. Clearer vision results in better decisions.

10. *Celebrate success.* You took the risk; now give yourself the reward. What's a compelling way to reward yourself? One of my friends is a sales rep and eBay fashion fan. He *loves* shopping online and getting good deals on designer duds. For a few hundred bucks he can buy a gorgeous designer suit. So for each sale he closes, he allots himself $100 toward an online shopping spree. That's motivation. On the days when he doesn't feel like prospecting (he hates cold calling), he'll look at his "watch list" of auction items in eBay for a few minutes of visual encouragement. That's enough to get him dialing again. He knows the celebration will make the work worth it.

COOL FREE RESOURCES

Go to www.RulesForRenegades.com and download "30 Days To Where You Want to Be," "Accountability Partner Worksheet," "Mastermind Group Worksheet," and "Goal Setting Worksheet."

Problems + Pain = Profit

Only Painful Problems Open Wallets

A pessimist sees the difficulty in every opportunity; an optimist sees the opportunity in every difficulty.

WINSTON CHURCHILL

THE WORLD IS ONE IMPERFECT PLACE. That's the good news. Every day new messes are created that require someone to come in and clean them up. Opportunities are all around you: pay attention! Learn to listen to someone who's in "business pain." Diagnose that pain first: perhaps the competition is crushing them, or markets haven't materialized, or their inefficient systems are stifling innovation. Then make sure the pain is perceived as a problem that needs a solution. *Problems + pain = profit.* The second step is key: only then will they open their wallets to get that pain removed.

I've created companies in two ways. The hard way is when I have no ideas, and I search for a problem to solve. I'll get to this shortly. The easy way is when a problem that needs solving pops right into my lap. As we saw in Chapter 1, the idea for Kuvera just dropped into my lap. Microsoft was feeling pain. The contractors like me were feeling pain. If I'd waited a week and a day, I'd have missed my chance to create the painkiller and compete with Volt. What did I learn from this experience?

1. *Pay attention.* Be on the lookout for opportunities. Make it a goal to be focused on seeing opportunities all around you. Then when one shows up, act on it.

2. *Stuff your feelings of fear or inadequacy.* So there's entrenched professional competition? You can provide something they don't. In the case of Kuvera and Microsoft, that meant treating the contractors like human beings as well as taking a lesser cut of their pay. Use whatever mind games you need to make yourself confident. For me, activating my deflector shield made me feel immune to Dick's attacks. My Confident Stance helped in Chapter 2 when I was dealing with Ryan's doubts about my abilities.

3. *Go for it.* When an opportunity pops into your lap, grab it. It doesn't matter if you're ready or not; you'll figure it out in time. You may get rejected; you may be wildly successful. You won't know unless you risk it. And what's to risk? I was starting with nothing and had this not worked out I would've ended with nothing. So I would have "lost" nothing!

What about when something doesn't fall into your lap? That was my next adventure; stay with me. I bought lists of Fortune 1000 information technology executives and started cold calling. I ground out code by day and dialed for dollars in the early morning and evening in my rent-an-office. I had huge bags under my eyes and was often too exhausted to hear the alarm each morning. In six months my fingers were raw meat from stabbing the phone buttons and my jaw was sore from nonstop pitching, but I'd sold services to five new clients.

Running with Scissors

My bank balance started growing, and I was finally clearing enough to break free from Microsoft. Just because I listened to the pain, I was suddenly the CEO of a profitable little company. So naturally I wanted to make it a profitable bigger company. I needed to expand beyond the services business, to develop products that had a higher profit margin. My company's assets—those Microsoft contractors—were high cost and fairly low profit. Plus, they walked out the door each day. I needed a product, something that I could sell a lot of with just a little overhead, something that scaled. I had found the problem, made sure it was painful, and now it was time for step three: to do something about it.

I moved to Northern California to be near more large corporations. I kept dialing for dollars, and in 1991 started a strategic consulting firm, Corporate Computing International (CCI), and folded Kuvera into it. CCI offered IT strategy and systems design consulting. We helped big companies design corporate software on more versatile PC platforms. Now I had a new executive-level business and could start charging the big bucks. I had to hire office staff, which set me back, and now CCI couldn't support me, so I had to get a day job contract programming at Apple Computer. Soon I was splitting my time between designing Apple's new manufacturing systems and calling information technology executives to nab some consulting gigs for the staff I'd acquired. I needed that new idea, and fast. I needed a product to sell.

Macintosh was getting its butt kicked by Windows 3.0 (the first version that didn't constantly crash), but I realized that Microsoft had a lot to learn from the friendly little fruit people. When Apple released the Macintosh, they provided a style guide, so people could design and develop software with consistent user interfaces. Now Microsoft was pushing Windows 3.0 on corporations worldwide with no style guide. Everyone was in a fever to embrace Bill's new baby, but these corporations were like first-time parents: they were thrilled but didn't quite know what to do with their new bundle of joy. Hey, I thought, here's an opportunity: I'll make a Dr. Spock for Windows users! This became our first product, GUI Guidelines.

So you see there's not that much difference between the easy and the hard way. Both ways require you to pay attention. The hard way requires more research and thought, but as I said, the world is one imperfect place. There's always something wrong somewhere. You just have look around and ask, "What's broken here? What needs to be fixed? What's missing?"

At this stage, I got my act together, sat down, and wrote out a detailed business plan, right? Wrong. Sometimes plans are overrated. As John Lennon put it, "Life is what happens while we're making other plans." In my career as an entrepreneur, angel investor, and venture capitalist, I've been closely involved in the start-ups of 36 companies to date. Of those 36, *not a single one* has executed its original business plan. Why? Because conditions changed. Competitors popped up, markets failed to materialize or mature, products didn't work as planned. You get the picture. When you're looking for investors, planning and clarifying your vision, or setting goals, you need a plan—we'll get to them shortly. But if the opportunity arises, start the business first and then plan where to take it. If you love and believe in your idea, you may just have to dive into it headfirst if a chance to fast-track presents itself.

Here's my business launching process: Three steps, then the void. Once you have your idea, figure out your first three steps, then get moving; the rest you'll work out in time. You figure out those first three steps by answering these questions:

1. How will you create your product or service?

2. How will you get the initial customers?

3. What will have to happen to take your company further?

I had my product, so, on to step two: customers. Who needed our Dr. Spock the most? The Fortune 1000, naturally. They had the most pain: they were converting their mainframe systems to run on PCs and were new to graphical environments. I had to move fast, because sooner or later Microsoft was going to catch on and try to crush my little company by providing its own style guide. It was murder closing sales. My competition came from the boys in the Big Six accounting firms, who told my prospective clients that they knew PC software development better than I did, which was bogus, but they talked a good game. That's the trouble with selling to the Fortune 1000; sometimes they play it too safe. There had to be a way around this. They had pain, and I was ready to remove it.

I'd made 500 cold calls, resulting in 35 meetings, all ending in outright rejection. I had what the clients needed. Why wouldn't they take a chance on me? After that thirty-fifth rejection, I vow to sit in my car until a solution surfaces. Moving my car to face the building entrance, I wait for my competitors to come out. Thirty minutes later, the I.T. manager who'd rejected me walks out with two guys—the competition. They're all smiles and handshakes. Grabbing my newspaper, I hold it in front of my face and peek around the edges at the three men. Their conversation drifts through my unrolled window.

"It's a good-news, bad-news situation," the I.T. manager says.

"Like watching your mother-in-law drive off a cliff—" says the first guy.

"—in your new BMW," adds the second guy.

Laughing, handshaking, backslapping ensue. Quite the chummy scene.

"Monday, 9 o'clock," the I.T. manager says. They all wave as he re-enters the building.

As my competitors walk past my car, I drop my newspaper and take a mental snapshot: middle-aged, cropped hair, navy blue suits, wedding bands, glasses. Their look says, "We're safe, professional, conservative. Hire us and your head won't roll." I'm single, still in my twenties, with long wild hair, and wearing Ross Dress for Less separates. My look says, "Paper or plastic?" or, if I've skimped on the makeup, "Want fries with that?" I get it now. Everything's an illusion. Time to try on a new one: conservative, established executive. I drive straight to the mall.

Armed with my new accoutrements (navy suit, glasses, wedding ring) and hair clipped under control, I resolve to rock my next sales call, lucky number 36.

. . .

Chevron's office is bright, airy, and redolent with the odor of burnt coffee. Bob Landon, the head of corporate information technology, urges me to "rush over" when I cold-call him. He quickly agrees to a one-day gig consulting on software design. Yes! Finally someone is taking a chance on me.

A week later, at the end of the consulting day, Bob shakes my hand. "Great job, Christine." He nods good-bye to the mostly male IT staff as they leave the conference room. Bob books another consulting day.

After the second successful gig, Bob leads me to his office for a powwow. "How 'bout that Montana?" he says.

"Some injury, eh?" I read the sports section of the newspaper now. Joe Montana, quarterback of the San Francisco 49ers at the time, was a god. I had learned how to worship.

"I'll say."

Once we reach his office, Bob's all business. "We need to train our team with more structure."

I remember what I learned from Bill Gates: sell it first, build it second. "How about a class, Bob? We just developed one." Well, I will develop one. After Bob buys it.

"Oh? How long is it?"

"About a day."

"Nine to five?"

I nod.

"Okay, we'll hold the first class on Monday. Set-up at eight?"

Ask for the order. "Okay." *You can't leave here without it.* "All I need is a purchase order."

"Right. Of course. How much?"

"How many students?"

"Twenty."

Hmm . . . how much to charge? What were those per-student costs in the Microsoft University class catalog? Can't remember. Okay, just guess. "So, at $300 per student we'll need $6,000."

"Hey, that's a terrific price."

Damn, too low. "I'm giving you a discount. We're testing this new class with your team."

Bob stands, smiling, and extends his hand: "$6,000 it is."

. . .

Thanks to my Mr. Coffee machine, I developed the course in a marathon weekend session. Finished it at 2 a.m. on Monday, and picked up the student materials at Kinko's four hours later—with just enough time to drive to Chevron.

Now that I had the right company, and a credible look, I could let my customers invent my product ideas for me by telling me their painful problems, and that's just what Chevron did.

Listening, Lattes, and Lightning Bolts

CCI thrived. We sold a *ton* of training and GUI Guidelines, and offered not only work group, department, and site licenses but also planetary licenses. That's when a huge conglomerate buys unlimited usage for all its sites. Microsoft bleated that I had no right to provide design standards for their product. Heck, they'd left their customers stranded, I'd simply provided the lifeboat. I offered them a planetary license for $300,000; they could be a customer just like everyone else. They bought and that worked—for a while. But I needed to get in front of more potential customers—and faster.

I cut a deal with a major training company and started offering public seminars on designing Windows software. The training company handled all the logistics and marketing, I provided the education, and we split the revenue. That is how I landed my first 100 of the Fortune 1000. Finally, I was successful enough to quit my gig at Apple. But I needed to do more. I landed a column at *PC Week,* and the exposure boosted our customer base to 300 of the Fortune 1000. Everything was going gangbusters, but I still kept my ear cocked for the next painful problem.

I didn't have to listen for long. Customers were begging for a guide to design distributed software applications, or client/server apps, which was the next big thing in corporate information technology. Corporations wanted to reduce their dependence on mainframe computers and embrace the rapid application development possible on PCs. We built a product called RADPath (Rapid Application Development Path) to show engineers how to design these PC-based corporate systems. We sold a bunch of that product too, because the big software companies hadn't created a methodology that was approachable and easy to use. Another painful problem solved—and 500 of the Fortune 1000 now served by CCI.

When I sold CCI four years after its inception, it was pushing $5 million in sales, with 700 of the Fortune 1000 as customers. It also gave me a crash course in thinking like a CEO, which is something that all of you, dear readers, need to start doing right away. Train yourself to both look at the big picture and to see that everything is an illusion. And of course, pick one that's empowering!

You'll benefit from cultivating an attitude that makes people want to open up to you, because listening is key to finding problems to diagnose and cure. In 1995, standing in line for coffee at Starbucks, I struck up a conversation with a guy who told me about the pain of marketing consumer products over the Internet. He knew there was an idea there but didn't understand the technology. I did. Within a few months the two of us had launched a company, planetU, that delivered personally targeted coupons and other promotions to customers. We raised venture capital financing, hired a rockin' team, and launched our Web-based service. Four years later I sold my shares to an investor group for a few million. The moral of the story is: Always talk to people when you're out in the world. You never know what it'll lead to: sometimes a new company, sometimes a new connection, sometimes a chance to make the world a little better.

Conversely, you can miss out on some fantastic opportunities when you clap your hands over your ears. One company I worked with was repeatedly asked by its customers for software that was easier to administer and monitor. Once the software was installed and customized, the customers complained that they had no choice but to hire expensive system administrators to maintain it. With a simple user interface and instructions in plainer English, they could have had one of their clerical workers sail the ship. But the company refused to listen to their pain. Soon their existing customers flocked to a competitor's product, and the pipeline for their budget-busting software dried up.

Another company I worked with was dead set on selling their product directly to telecommunications carriers, who are notoriously slow in decision making and can have serious Not-Invented-Here syndrome, meaning that since they didn't think of it, it can't be any good. To make matters worse, the vice president of sales insisted on targeting the top telecommunications companies, who were fat and happy. Fat and happy customers already know they don't have to Dumpster-dive for their next meal; they keep their well-fed butts planted. Meanwhile, several midsized and smaller companies were feeling pain and actually asking to purchase the product—but the company didn't even bother to return their calls! When the board grew concerned about the excruciatingly slow climb up the sales ramp, the VP of sales and CEO both pooh-poohed its concerns, saying, "These accounts simply take time," and expanded the sales focus to the top automobile manufacturers, another target market that already had a solution and wasn't in pain. The company eventually ran out of money and the financiers lost confidence in the rigid (and unsuccessful) sales approach. To add insult to injury, a competitor popped up and sold their similar solution to midsized telecom companies as well as to embattled smaller ones.

When Your Brain Won't Storm: Mind Maps

With Kuvera and CCI, I paid attention to the pain of the marketplace and moved fast to reduce it. I didn't have to search too hard to find my next round of customers, though I did work harder than ever to take my business to the next level. However, we've all had times when we hit a creative roadblock or have a solution in search of a problem. When I want to develop ideas for a product or service, or to plan a particular goal, I create a mind map. It's a great way to prime the idea pump.

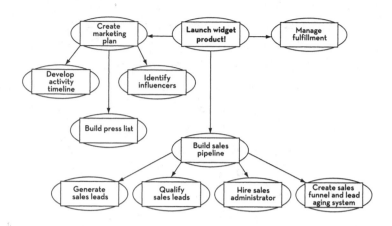

Here's how to make one:

1. Get a poster-sized piece of paper or a whiteboard and draw a circle the size of a Peppermint Pattie in the middle. Write what you want to achieve with your product or service in the middle, for example, "Launch widget product." This is your primary goal.

2. Draw spokes around your primary goal circle, and attach a circle to each spoke. Label these circles with activities that will help you achieve your primary goal, for instance, "Create marketing plan," "Build sales pipeline," "Manage fulfillment."

3. For each activity, again draw spokes from the circle and attach additional circles to them, labeling the spokes with activities or ideas that would support them. For example, for "Build sales pipeline," you might have circles that say "Generate sales leads," "Qualify sales leads," "Hire sales administrator,"

"Create sales funnel and lead aging system," and many more. For "Create marketing plan," you might have circles that say "Build press list," "Develop activity timeline," "Identify influencers," and, of course, many more.

4. Keep drawing spokes and circles until you've run out of ideas for each activity. Then highlight the most important ones, and start executing them. You'll get to them all in time.

Check out MindJet.com for free mind mapping software.

How to Create a Killer Business Plan with the Three Cs

You've probably noticed that I'm a frequent flyer when it comes to seat-of-the-pants travel. Gutting it out usually works for me. If I'd stopped to draw up a meticulous business plan before launching Kuvera, the business would never have happened. With CCI, I had tactical, shoot-from-the-hip product plans and an overall loose business strategy so I could communicate the company's direction and goals to my team. I never needed a business plan because I didn't need to attract investors to underwrite it, and because my business was so basic that it was easy to communicate my vision to our team. Conversely, when launching planetU, my partner and I opted to get outside investors. We developed a business plan from the very beginning and a fairly lame (but colorful) pretty-picture prototype so the investors could visualize how the system would look to the consumers. We also had five-year financials with projected revenues and costs. With those in hand, we were able to raise $2.5 million by selling one-third of our company. *To get the serious bucks you need a serious business plan.* And if you're an intrapreneur, the same applies when proposing a corporate project, new approach, or strategic alliance. See this as your "company" in the examples that follow.

Once you have the idea, package it well. The way you present your company and vision determines whether you get the right financial partners (or budget approval), most favorable financing terms, most outstanding executives, most committed customers, and the best shot at success. Life is marketing, and your business plan, executive summary, and financing pitch are the ultimate marketing tools.

Your business plan will be about 20 pages, covering all aspects of your business (see "How to Do It" below). The executive summary is a two- to five-page bottom-line version of your business plan, a riveting bulletin from the front line that primes investors to read on. Few people will want to pour over the whole plan. This is why you've got to rope them in with those first pages and establish that you're a savvy, trustworthy person with a substantial idea before you lay out all the details. The financing pitch is 10 to 15 PowerPoint slides extracted from the executive summary. This is the distillation of your business, which you'll design to deliver in about 20 minutes for attention-span-challenged people.

I'm amazed at how many entrepreneurs and intrapreneurs recognize the importance of packaging themselves well, yet repeatedly miss the opportunity to market their business effectively. A big part of the problem is the love-hate relationship we have with business plans.

As a former venture capitalist and current entrepreneur and business consultant, I've read more business plans and project proposals than I care to remember. Often the plans were for products or services that no one truly needed, or projects that weren't cost justified. What, the world wasn't waiting for that combination nail polish—wallpaper stripper? The expansion to the manufacturing plant was optional after all? Sometimes the plans were for great ideas but were presented poorly. What a shame to have a brilliant idea and a brilliant way to execute it, only to capsize it with a lackluster business plan or financing pitch. To shine, your plan needs to be concise, compelling, and complete.

BE CONCISE

A *concise* plan provides a simple explanation for why your business is a great idea, and how you'll execute the steps to pull it off. Do you stick with a novel if it doesn't grab you in the first few pages? Me neither. No matter how polished your prose, few of your potential financiers will read the plan in its entirety. Your goal is to explain your company in such a crisp and sexy way that the money contingent won't be able to put it down. You must convince them that you have a basic execution strategy and pragmatic tactics for making your vision a reality. More on this at the end of the chapter.

BE COMPELLING

A *compelling* opportunity is the one that has the right deal, with the right price, at the right time, with the right product or service and the right team. Compelling deals *always* get financed with favorable terms. The goal is to make your company appear to be deeply compelling. To uncover your "compelling quotient" answer the following questions:

- What, specifically, do you think is compelling about your business (look at your products or services, team, unique approach, intellectual property, etc.)?

- Does your product or service clearly define and address a painful problem (or, in some cases, a key social trend)?

- Has your team had prior start-up success so investors know that they're taking a bet on a proven pony?

- Do you have high-profile advisory board members?

- Have you already attracted either paying

customers or those who have signed on for a free
trial?

- Are your financial projections aggressive but
  realistic?

- Are your target markets tangible and accessible?

- Could your product or service lead to an
  expanded line of additional offerings?

- Have you built solid strategic partnerships?

- Do you have diverse and low-cost sales channels?

- Are you creating profound intellectual property?

- Most important, does your product or service
  have the kind of sex appeal that will make
  everyone in your target market want it?

Be Complete

You *must* have a trusted third party review your plan
to ensure it addresses all possible issues an investor
might have. "Friendly fire" feedback is essential before
you pitch to the less friendly folks. Ask anyone who can
help—your start-up-savvy attorney, advisory board,
mentors, and friends who have expertise in the specific
market you are addressing or in business overall—to
punch holes in your plan. Give them a list of questions
to answer, such as: What do you think our business is?
Is it interesting to you—why or why not? Were you to

consider investing in it, what additional information would you need? This is a time to lay bare any wobbly or weak aspects of your plan, when you've got time to fix them.

One of the roles of a business plan is to show how capable you are, that you've thought through all the issues. It's helpful to include statements that illustrate where you'll take the business once some milestones have been achieved. Financiers want to believe that you understand the key issues associated with building your company and that you are prepared for the challenge. If you charge ahead with an incomplete plan, such as one that lacks detailed financials, or a marketing or sales strategy, or a specific product plan, you'll look either unprofessional, fly-by-night, or both. Be *complete*—it will help you gain the trust of all who read your plan.

If you're a *South Park* fan, you'll remember the episode called "Underpants Gnomes." These gnomes have built a business based on stealing underpants from the residents of South Park. When the kids finally catch them and ask why they are doing this, the gnomes say it's all part of their business plan. "What's your plan, exactly?" the kids ask. One of the gnomes fires up a PowerPoint presentation to outline their three-phase approach. Slide no. 1 says "Steal Underpants." Slide no. 2 is blank. Slide no. 3 says "Profit!"

I cannot stress how many business plans I've seen like this, where phase one is "Create widget," phase three is "Profit!" and the crucial phase two is a complete unknown. See "Applying the Three Cs" at the end of this chapter for the details you'll need in your business or project plan.

A Lesson

Here's a sample paragraph from an executive summary I read several years ago.

Freight trucks in America travel 30 billion miles empty each year. This inefficiency costs distributors hundreds of millions of dollars in unnecessary freight handling costs, such as scheduling one-way trips and paying for last-minute loads. Our browser-based software matches empty containers with loads that need to be moved nationwide. By using our software, distributors and manufacturers can save millions of dollars in the first year of use alone. The distributors and manufacturers are under extreme pressure from their executive management to reduce their inefficient freight costs by 10 percent annually for the next three years. Our team of seasoned freight, distribution, and manufacturing executives think we can capture a minimum of 1 percent of the market over the next three years. This would result in profitability six months into year two, growth of over 100 percent per year, and based on industry-standard P/E ratios, a valuation of over $200 million at the end of year three.

Wow! Huge pain, customers empowered to remove it, the right team to make it happen, and the potential for a glorious exit. Concise? Yes! Compelling? Yes! What's not to like? The entrepreneurs missed the "complete" part. They fell apart in both their business plan and in presentations when they tried to detail exactly how they would execute on this fantastic opportunity. They sought capital for over a year and never got funded.

Meanwhile, several other companies had identified this problem + pain dynamic duo. They popped up with similar ambitions and actual strategies they could execute and financiers could believe. The front-runner never even got into the race. They had jumped into the starting position without being ready and were already dusted before the race began.

How to Do It

So, now you're ready to create a killer business plan, which will yield a killer executive summary and a killer financing pitch. Put in the hours to make it perfect, because you'll be repurposing the content in sales presentations, marketing collateral and white papers, recruiting pitches, and your Web site.

Here's how to do it. Using the sample business plan outline from the Resources section at the end of this chapter, begin to fill in each section. Do *not* use a business plan package. Using these fill-in-the-blanks business plans hangs a big sign on your back that says: "Dis me.

I've never done this before!" Here are the key risks fin-anciers worry about:

- People (Have you hired the right ones?)

- Product or service (Can you build and deliver it? Will it fly?)

- Market (Is it big enough? Can you reach it?)

- Financial (How much will it cost us?)

You won't be able to eliminate the financial risk completely, so focus on showing how solid your people are, how exceptional your product or service is (and why), and how huge the market you're going after is and how you'll capture it. You *must* define your current and potential competitors too, in honest, realistic terms. Remember, your plan needs to reduce your investors' fear of risk and increase their greed for gain.

The sample business plan outline will help you ar-ticulate why your company is a winner in a concise, compelling, and complete way. When pitching investors (or customers or the press, for that matter), you'll want to e-mail a list of the top five qualities that make your company compelling. This will increase your likelihood of catching their eyes and getting them to read your ex-ecutive summary.

You'll also need a financial model. Be sure to make it interactive, which means it will be formula based and take longer to create than a basic static model. But trust me, you will definitely change your financial projections, so provide for flexibility from the get-go. An interactive model will also help you address "what-if" scenarios. Chances are good that potential financiers will slash your first-year revenue projections in half. What repercussions will this have? Run it through the model and find out.

Your business plan isn't cast in stone; it's more like wobbling in Jell-O. Write it to clarify your thoughts, then be willing to modify it, sometimes radically, or even toss it. Here's the secret: *everyone* is making it up as they go along. The point is to be flexible with all your plans. Your dessert topping sucks? Maybe it's a terrific floor wax.

Yes, anarchy and chaos create opportunity, and it's all around us. You have a choice when you find yourself immersed in a world of problems that are painful. You can duck and run for cover, or you can listen and leap to find the cure. Go find the profit behind the painful problems!

APPLYING THE THREE Cs: BE CONCISE, COMPELLING, COMPLETE

In order for your business plan to be concise, compelling, and complete you'll want to include the following elements:

- A quantifiable explanation of the painful problem and how you plan to solve it

- Your company's objectives, including an analysis of the competition

- A description of your product or service, how you plan to achieve world domination with it, and which follow-on products you have in mind to up-sell to customers

- Five years' worth of financials (quarterly for the first three, annually is okay for years four and five) and how you plan to cover growth and expenses

- Marketing and sales strategy, defining your pricing, product positioning, promotions, and the like (at the least a section describing the first few releases of a product and the high-level product plan)

- Your team, and why they are exceptional

- Your plan for overcoming predictable obstacles—for example,, risk management and mitigation

- Everything included in the "Sample Business Plan outline" and "Pitch Critique Template" (www.Rules ForRenegades).

- Check out "Effective Board Reporting" (www.Rules ForRenegades). These are the statistics you'll need

(continues)

to track to stay on top of your business. You might as well include projections for these in your plan.

Include only the information necessary to support the claims you make in the plan. Appendixes, which might include résumés of the key executives, press coverage, white papers, or anything else to boost credibility, are extra. If you're tempted to be more long-winded, imagine FedEx dumping yet another load of documents onto a busy financier's desk, where they'll join the already tottering stack of business plans. There are some slim, sexy Boxsters there, and then there's your big, clunky minivan. Which plans do you think the investor will grab first?

COOL FREE RESOURCES

Go to www.RulesForRenegades.com and download "Mind Map Template," "How to Position Your Product or Service," "ROI-Focused Sales," "Lead Generation & Qualification," "Lead Qualification Roadmap," "Sample Business Plan Outline," "Effective Board Reporting," "Product Design," and "Pitch CritiqueTemplate."

Build Power Instead of Borrowing It

Attempting World Domination in Bill Gates's Bedroom

Nothing external to you has any power over you.

RALPH WALDO EMERSON

Y OU'RE THE CEO of your own life, and maybe even of your own business, so you often have to deal with power. As we go through life and meet people, we learn about power—who has it and who doesn't. You'll always be dealing with people who have power over you, to some extent, but I want you to be able to have power too—to know where it starts and where it stops, and to exercise it responsibly and compassionately over others. But how do you get it? And what, exactly, is it? Is it money? Is it position? Is it the ability to influence? I learned most about it by seeking out, and hanging out with, powerful people.

S ubject: "If you donate to the AIDS Action Committee, you'll win dinner with a fabulous blonde!"

I press "Send" and the e-mail is on its way to the intended target. I'm the blonde bait; Bill Gates is the big fish. My office-mate Frank, at Lotus Development Corporation, has done so much for me: made me over, taught me to apply makeup, and now many of his friends are sick with AIDS. Some are dying. I need to help, and asking a billionaire for a small contribution to a worthy cause seems the least I can do. And besides, how cool would that be? To bag a donation from a billionaire? Maybe even have dinner together? I've only met Bill once, and I doubt he'll remember me. He probably won't answer. But it's worth a shot.

Moments later a reply pops onto my screen. "How much?"

Whoa! I take a deep breath and type "One thousand dollars, paid to AIDS Action Committee, sent to me via FedEx," and press Send again. The next day there's an orange and purple envelope in my mail slot. Inside is a personal check from Bill Gates for $1,000. It even has his home address on it.

"You should've asked for a million!" squeals Frank, grabbing the check and heading for the photocopier. The constant *vooowoosh voowoosh* says he's making a ton of copies for his friends.

A thank-you e-mail, without specifying a date for the dinner, keeps me off the hook for a while. Heck, I'm now in Massachusetts, Bill's across the country in Washington. He probably won't follow through anyway. With the check passed along to the AAC I promptly forget the whole thing.

· · ·

Months later my contract at Lotus is up. I hear rumblings from Redmond that the next version of Windows (3.0) will be all we engineers have dreamed of. I pitch myself via phone to the new head of Windows and lock in a programming gig. One day, after only a few months back at Microsoft, I get an e-mail with the subject: "I found you." The message: "I believe you owe me dinner. How's tonight?"

Yikes. Bill Gates has called my bluff. Why did I offer myself up in the first place? It seemed like a fun idea, but now that it's time to actually follow through, I must admit I want to be near him, to find out what a billionaire is like one-on-one. Will he spout words of business wisdom? Will he offer to become my mentor?

I want to reply, but my fingers are numb, my stomach's in knots, and my skin's indecisive—icy and sweating at the same time—and things look kind of blurry. Stop. Do something you know how to do from all that time as a monk. Use a relaxation mantra. Close your eyes, still your mind, meditate. Ready.

"OK, want me to come by your office?"

The response comes instantly. "No, your cardkey won't let you into my building. I'll come to you."

"What time?"

"Seven OK?"

"Sure."

"See you then."

At Microsoft, the primary form of communication is e-mail, secondary is voice mail, tertiary is face mail, meaning you actually engage in a conversation with a fellow human being. We nerds avoid social contact at all costs.

I hope, I *pray*, that in two hours Bill will come directly to my office, instead of schmoozing his way down the hall talking to all the guys. If they find out I'm having dinner with him, they'll assume it's a date. As a technical woman at Microsoft your social position is precarious: if you date company guys, you're a slut; if you don't, you're a bitch. I learned this the first time I worked here. I didn't date the guys in Systems where I worked, so I was a bitch. I dated the guys in Applications, a few buildings away, so I was a slut. This time I'd promised myself I would skip Microsoft guys altogether.

Time speeds past as I fix an infinite loop and find a null pointer. At seven o'clock sharp Bill's tousled blonde head pops into my office. "Hey, Christine."

"Hey, Bill."

"Nice poster." He nods toward the "My First Million" poster tacked to the off-white wall. It shows a million dollars loosely piled in the shape of a pyramid. I ordered it from *Inc.* magazine as a tool to help me focus on my goal: having my own company, being free one day from the wage-slave world.

"Oh, yeah, it's a goal of mine."

"Yeah?"

"Yeah, you know, to make a million dollars. I mean, not just one million, many millions, but you've got to start somewhere, so one million seemed to be logical. . . ."

"Hungry?" Bill points his head out the door.

"Kind of." I head into the hallway, Bill's a few feet ahead of me. Please God, please let the guys be in their offices. Please.

They aren't. They're lining the corridor, like they're waiting for a parade. And I'm in it. As we walk through the staring mob, Bill asks too loudly, "Can you drive me home after dinner?"

"Um, okay." From the corner of my eye I see the guys elbowing each other, some leering, some snickering. Bill's not walking fast enough. The stairwell is a few yards ahead; the elevator is way across the lobby. Waiting for the elevator will be excruciating with all these eyes drilling holes in my head.

Bill wants to chat. "So, I thought we'd have dinner . . . do you like Thai food? Then we could hang out at my place and . . ."

"Stairs," I say, sliding before him. "Let's take the stairs," I hurl the door open and lunge down to the parking lot.

It's dusk as my blue Mazda Miata zooms across the bridge to Seattle. Bill guides me to one of his favorite Thai restaurants.

As we peruse the menu, Bill appears calm. I'm twitchy . . . but trying to be cool. "So, what's good here?"

"Oh, everything. I mean, all the chicken and fish stuff. I don't eat meat."

"Really?" *Ah, a subject I can actually talk about. Maybe even a potential bond.*

"Yeah, I thought it would be cool to avoid something because I want to. You know, kind of a willpower exercise." This is the man who leveraged the crappy Altair computer into a booming business. Management says next year, 1990, Microsoft will hit $1 billion in sales. No software company has done this yet, but I'm betting on Bill. I don't really think he needs to enhance his willpower.

As dinner progresses I start to worry a little more. Bill's a paradox: compassionate and cocky, genuine and arrogant, grown-up and elfin all at once. This little elf runs a software powerhouse that's taking on the world, one software company at a time. This little elf has an arsenal of weapons to squash his competition. Lotus was a threat with its market-leading spreadsheet, then *boom!* Microsoft smashed them. WordPerfect was a threat with its market-leading word processing software, then *boom!* Microsoft smashed them too. Now the company is aiming for IBM. *IBM.* They're, like, enormous. They're, well, IBM for Chrissakes. I'm fascinated. I'm afraid. What if I actually end up liking him? He's a Microsoft guy, he holds all the cards, he can't be as nice as he seems. Yep, liking him would definitely be a bad thing.

"Hey! Can I drive home?"

"Um, okay." I hand the keys to Bill.

"Super!" We jump in just as it starts to rain. "We need driving music, something lively." I grope in the glove box, find Madonna's latest CD, *Like a Prayer*, pop it in, relax in the bucket seat. I feel better having Bill behind the wheel. I bet the Microsoft shareholders do, too. We tear down the highway, with the rain obscuring the taillights before us. "This is fun, it's like a little toy car," Bill hollers over the slapping rain. He's driving too fast for the poor visibility. I grip the dashboard as the car hydroplanes to the right.

We pull up to Bill's middle-class suburban home. It's stunning: it's ordinary. It probably has three bedrooms, and it's surprisingly light on curb appeal; you'd never know a billionaire lives here. You wouldn't even think a millionaire did.

Inside, Bill turns to me with a bright face. "Hey! Today IBM endorsed Microsoft Windows in front of the world, and today I found out you're the first female contract engineer we've hired without a college diploma . . . or even a high school one. Let's celebrate!" He swings open the fridge, revealing a dozen neatly stacked bottles of Dom Perignon.

I don't remember discussing my education at dinner. Maybe I forgot? Or was Bill checking me out? Is that good—or creepy? "What about OS/2?" I'd pounded away on that operating system the last time I worked at Microsoft. Was my work wasted?

"It's IBM's now. We're going to make Windows the desktop standard." Just like that. Bill seems certain of it.

"We better tell Lotus, Adobe, WordPerfect, all those guys who're developing apps for OS/2."

"We will. Don't worry." Pop! Bill uncorks the champagne like a pro. He has lots of reasons to celebrate. It's 1989. Microsoft has swelled to 4,000 employees worldwide, just a few years after going public. And IBM, in its infinite brilliance, has just handed Bill the keys to the desktop.

This is the first billionaire bachelor pad I've ever seen. From the standard-issue 1980s kitchen to the living room with low-slung couches, assorted surfaces are festooned with small yellow sticky notes, fluttering like tiny canaries. Scribbled with suggestions or reminders, each one chirps for attention. "Let's replace this coffee table." "A brown rug would suit this room."

"Why the sticky notes?" I call from living room to kitchen.

"Oh. They're from my mom," his voice comes back softer. I can hear the fondness, the mother-melt. Then a hint of *Gosh, I wish she hadn't seen that.* "Just her ideas and stuff."

Continuing my tour, I walk down a short hallway and—voilà! Bill's bedroom. Whoa! What's this? A whiteboard! Bill's standing behind me. He'd snuck up, Ninja-like. "My mom lists things, and just like in Windows, I check what I want. See: do I want any new suits? If yes, I check the box she drew next to the colors I want. Do I want to host a Christmas party? I fill in the radio button: yes or no?"

O-kay... "Well, uh, I mean, it's a superefficient way to communicate. I mean, if she's in your house a lot." I want to compliment them both, but I'm kind of weirded out.

"Hey—I do puzzles really fast."

Thank God, a topic change. "Oh?"

"Yeah. There's one in the kitchen that says the fastest it's ever been assembled is seven minutes. *Seven.* Can you believe that? I can do it in four minutes, sometimes even less. You can take it apart and time me!" He's beckoning me toward the kitchen.

By this time, I'd witnessed countless attempts by nerds to impress me. Heck, I even had my own stupid nerd tricks I did to impress the guys. Burping the alphabet was my specialty. Think I'll skip that one tonight. "Um, I believe you, Bill, really.

You're a supersmart guy. Why don't we just talk? And where's that champagne?"

Bill returns from the kitchen, and hands me a glass of golden bubbles as we settle on the couch. We gulp in silence, and he refills both glasses. A soothing calm overcomes me as my limbs loosen. "So, Truth or Dare?" I offer.

"Truth. Yeah, truth."

I would've thought he'd go for the dare. "All right, what's your deepest fear?"

"That's easy," He replies immediately, no thought required. "Not getting smarter. Did you know that after 30, you just stop getting smarter? And then you get older, and well, it's downhill from there."

"Wow." I never worry about not getting smarter. I worry about more pressing issues, like my job debugging the Windows Software Development Kit. And I really worry about the poor guys debugging Windows itself. Now *that* is a job that *really* sucks. "So, what's your plan?"

"Surround myself with smart people. As I get older, keep bringing in more young, smart people, so the intelligence at Microsoft will increase as the median age does."

"Wow." This guy has a plan for everything. "Do you think your plan will succeed?"

"Yes. Of course." Bill is surprised I've questioned him.

"How do you know? I mean, can you plan all aspects of life? Like what about miracles and stuff? Those are unplanned. How do you explain them?"

"There are no miracles. You can explain everything, *everything*, with physics. The universe is like a big plan."

Again I see the expression of supreme confidence, of resolution, of *knowing*, on his face. This guy has an answer for everything. Better skip the God topic; that might be depressing. "So, do you, ummm, have a plan for your life?"

"Yeah, sure. Get married in a few years, at around 40 have a few kids, take Microsoft to the next level."

"You know all that? Now?" Hey, sooner or later his mom will want grandkids. Maybe she'll put up a few sticky notes and off to the altar he'll go.

"Oh, c'mere! I want to show you something." Bill takes my hand, leads me to the kitchen. "You need to see these. Tell me what you think." On the dining table are models of three homes. Not homes, really, not mansions, not even estates, but *compounds*. "So when I get married, and start having kids, well, this is the home I'm having built for them."

"Wow."

"So these are the finalists. I had a competition among these top architects, and I need to pick one. All of the designs are super. Here, I'll walk you through them." We pull up chairs, and he spends the next 30 minutes explaining the details that'll be in the house regardless of design, followed by the specifics of each model. "Okay, now you're well informed. Which do you like best?"

"This one." I point to option two. "It's less extreme, like a normal house that grew really, really big."

"Normal's good. I want my kids to grow up feeling normal, not with a huge house and servants and stuff like that."

"Bill, all of these homes are huge, and your kids, they won't have normal lives." He frowns, slouching in the chair. Did he really think they would? "I mean, you're rich, you're famous; you should enjoy that, and your kids should reap the benefits. But this house, the one we're in right now, this is normal. These models, they're not normal, Bill. Not normal at all."

"Yeah. I mean, I know. Guess I just thought they'd be super-normal, but still kinda normal." He's tapping model number 2 with his right pointer finger, gazing down at the table. His face shows his disappointment that he can't have fame and fortune *and* a low-profile middle-class life. Maybe no one has been as blunt as I have been.

"No," I say. "I'm sorry." And I am. Because I understand. All his life he wanted to be normal, to be accepted, to fit in, and in his quest he surpassed his goal and became supernormal, super-accomplished, and now he'll never be normal, not ever.

Bill straightens up, smiles. "So, another bottle of champagne?"

"No, I've got to go." I look away. I'm different from Bill, but my need is the same. I too was a misfit who wanted so badly to fit in, find my place, but I never could, and it makes me both sad and resolute because this is who I am, and there's some good to it. At least that's what I want to think.

"Please. Don't go yet." He's not ready to be alone with all these feelings. He's using his elfin look, with the tipped grin, big pleading eyes.

"Maybe just a few minutes." *You know, a few blond highlights would really look good on him. Maybe shape his eyebrows a little too, and get new glasses. Needs wardrobe work, but he's definitely got potential.* This time, I'm the one with the plans. I have big ones for Bill and me. Big.

. . .

A month later I get an e-mail entitled "Merry Christmas." It's from Bill. "My life is really complicated right now. I'd like to see you again. Beginning of the year OK?" We've exchanged friendly e-mails, so at least I didn't blow it. No harm in waiting a little longer for our next date. Ohmygod. It was a date, wasn't it?

It ends up being a *lot* longer—March 17—when we get together next. Clear-skinned on our last date, I now have an icky bout of stress-related adult acne. If I ask for a rain check Bill will forget about me, probably never ask me out again. Someone more interesting will come around and I'll be "Christine who?" I'd better say yes. Leaning into the mirror I hear Frank's first rule of makeup application: "less is more, else you look like a whore." But I can't use less and cover these pimples. So I layer it on. *Thick.*

Hey, I can do this, hang with the rich and famous. Piece of cake. Those self-improvement tapes are working. Yes, Brian Tracy, I am *Thinking Big*. And yes, Zig Ziglar, I've got a *View from the Top* and it is deeee-licious. Oh, yeah.

Everything's cool until we arrive at the dining room of the Columbia Tower Club, high atop a Seattle skyscraper. The maître d', the patrons, the busboys, *everyone* is staring at us. It's unnerving. But still I make it through dinner, through the disco, through the comedy club.

The next morning I sneak out of bed, freshen up my makeup, tiptoe across the light shag carpet back to Bill's bed.

"Good morning." Bill sighs, smiling with closed eyes.

"'Morning," I reply, speed dressing, eager for my escape. I don't want him to see my face—my acne ran rampant last night. "Well, thanks. Bye."

Bill throws on a tan terrycloth robe and follows me to the door. He's still standing on his porch as I peel out of the driveway. As soon as he fades from my rearview mirror I smear the inch of makeup off my face.

Two weeks. No call from Bill.

· · ·

After a few months it's clear: I've been dumped. I was like a dog chasing a car—there was no way I'd catch it, and all I did was look dumb and get hurt. Frank thinks otherwise. He says, "Honey, you darted the morning after. Everyone knows the darter is the dumper." I object but Frank insists, saying, "What was he supposed to do? Beg for you back with a humiliating phone call? He's Bill Gates, for Chrissakes."

———————

I started out wanting to raise money for AIDS, which led to dinner, which became a date, which resulted in my losing sight of why I wanted to hang with Bill in the first place: to learn from him. Many of us fall into a familiar trap: we choose power/money/self-esteem-by-association because we don't think we can create our own. We think we'll get a "contact high" from being close to power instead of by wielding it ourselves. Then we're left powerless when the relationship goes south, the association withers, or the bank balance plunges. What kind of power do you want in your life and over your life? Do you want power by association—with someone or some place? Or do you want to build your own power? We can't rock in business and life until we untangle that relationship, claim our power, and start creating with it. Make the choice now to have your own power, money, self-esteem. Then no one can take it away.

One thing, though, struck me, stuck with me: Bill's supreme confidence, his certainty that he'd achieve what he set out to do. His ability to create his world, to influence outcomes—that's what power came to mean to me. *And as I watch more closely now, from a distance, I realize that power isn't something bestowed on a person due to wealth or position, but that it comes from that inner confidence.* Having that confidence puts one in a particular position, which people respond to. I decided to try on that illusion, adopt that sense of knowing that I'd get what I wanted. My study guide became *Fortune* magazine, where I read about powerful executives and tried to glean how they got that way. I embraced external evidence of power: the suits, the stature; I was trying to be like Bill.

And it was working. I wrote a letter to a particularly fascinating man and we ended up spending some time together. I didn't sleep with this second billionaire, I wasn't ready. What's the rush? When he asked me to meet him in a location that required me to miss some key business meetings, I said no. He persisted, offering to send his plane for me. I declined as gracefully as possible; I simply couldn't be his beck-and-call-girl. I'd learned my lesson. But he did have the same supreme self-confidence that Bill had. It was almost intoxicating.

Enchiladas and the Internet

Life has its challenges, and five years later my confidence got wobbly again. I was the target of an ugly public attack, which you'll read more about in Chapter 5. Although I'd learned lots about how to act like I had power, and even how to gain it and use it, a big part of me was still looking for power outside of myself, forgetting the lessons I learned from Bill. My sense of power was wrapped up with my company, and then that company was gone once I sold it. A friend offered an intriguing diversion: an introduction to Larry Ellison of Oracle. I thought maybe he would provide a boost to my self-confidence and self-esteem.

———

Larry was supposed to call me from the lobby of the Santa Clara Marriott at 6 p.m. Then I'd meet him and we'd go from there. It's 6:15 p.m. No call. Then 6:30 p.m. Nada. It's 7 p.m. when I remember the only other time I'd been stood up: for the high school prom by Jimmy. Jimmy the stoner and Larry the businessman blend into one. And I hate him. Hate him for making me feel so ugly, so undesirable, so . . . *optional*. Does he think he can get away with this? I call his office and get voice mail.

"Hi, Larry, it's Christine Comaford. We had dinner plans tonight. But I'm still here, at the hotel, and you're . . . well, I don't know where. Look, I don't care that you're a billionaire. I've dated them before, so it's not like I'm impressed by your wealth or anything. I wanted to meet you because I thought you might be a fascinating person. Well, a fascinating person with no manners? *Not* fascinating." I hang up, strip, jump into the shower.

Thirty minutes later my skin is prunelike as I step from the shower. The red message light on the hotel phone flashes.

"Christine, this is Larry. There was a mix-up. My calendar says we're on for tomorrow night—my assistant and I must've had a miscommunication. I'm so sorry. I don't stand up women. Please call me tonight. Any time." He leaves his home phone number.

My personal digital assistant has two home phone numbers for my other failed relationships with billionaires. Am I really going to try this again? Another 30 minutes pass, and I decide to call him back. Just a quick call. Just to get closure before I walk away.

"Hi, Larry, it's Christine Comaford."

"Oh, hi, thanks for calling. I'm so sorry. Please understand this was simply a scheduling error . . ."

"Yeah, well . . ."

"Give me another chance. Are you still in town tomorrow night?"

"Yes, but . . ."

"I'll make it worth it. Hey," he laughs, "I'll even be your man slave for the evening. How can you refuse an offer like that?"

"Well, that *is* tempting . . ."

"Great. I'll pick you up at 6:30 p.m. tomorrow night at the Marriott."

"Okay, but let's make it casual attire. Jeans."

"Jeans. Deal. See you tomorrow."

. . .

He picks me up in a $5,000 Brioni suit. Jeans, *right*. I should have worn a business suit. I would have been more confident in my clothing armor. We zoom from the entryway—he didn't even use the parking lot—in his silver Acura NSX. He says he's driven all the best cars on the planet, and this one handles so much better than the Ferrari Diablo. Gotcha. I'll remember that the next time I'm car shopping.

To his credit, Larry changes into khakis and a T-shirt shortly after we arrive at his samurai estate in Atherton, California. He's in the kitchen, says he's cooking dinner, but refuses to let me keep him company. Is that the crinkling sound of tin foil? Did his housekeeper make dinner? Is he just heating it up? Does it matter?

After chicken enchiladas, Larry says, "Hey, I want to show you something. It's the future." He jumps up from the table and leads me to the upstairs den. It's a steep flight of stairs, and he's ahead of me. His khakis cling to his perfectly sculpted tush. "Okay, so the Internet . . . it's the next big thing."

"Uh-huh." A fit nerd . . . *this* is a first.

"It's going to change everything. *Everything*."

"Sounds cool." Top of the stairs. Dang! There goes my view.

"It's like one huge database that everyone can tap in to, effortlessly." Larry walks over to a TV set and stands before it.

"Everyone?" Wow, I didn't notice the muscle definition in his shoulders, arms, chest. This guy must work out. *A lot.*

"Yes, consumers could shop online, research medical info, interact with others of similar interests. Employees could access their insurance benefits, salespeople could track their quarterly sales. All this self-serve data, empowering people.

And this," he pats a VCR-like device on top of the TV set, "this is going to make it all happen."

Another billionaire, another nerd trick, another attempt to impress. Bill wanted me to time him assembling a jigsaw puzzle; Larry wants me to watch a software demo. I want to scream, "Hey! I'm impressed already! You're a titan of industry, and you're sexy, and your body is spectacular! I'm impressed! I swear!"

Larry turns on the TV, pushes a button on the little box. "This set-top box turns your average TV into an Internet access point. This is going to blow you away."

We stare in silence at the blank screen.

He fiddles with the knobs, cables, power cord. "Okay, there. This is going to blow you away."

We stare in silence at the blank screen.

"Hmmmm. Something's not working. It worked yesterday . . . "

"I'm sure it's really cool, Larry."

We exchange e-mails several days a week. He's witty and charming. He even e-mails me a haiku he wrote about hiking Half Dome—did I inspire him? I have Carson's Ribs, his favorite, FedExed from Chicago to his office in California. He's fun and smart and seems a little vulnerable beneath it all.

We talk on the phone after he returns from Hong Kong. "What was the coolest thing about your trip?"

"The watches. I got a few more Patek Philippes. They're *gorgeous*. The jewelry, too. Enormous, perfect diamonds, emeralds, you name it."

"Oh, I'm not really into rocks," I say.

"*You will be.*" And he sounds like the Silicon Valley version of Yoda. I swear. And I get it then. Rocks. Rocks will be in my future. From him? For me? Wow! So soon?

A few dates later I decide to impress him. I plan a romantic day at the fabulous Meadowood resort in Napa Valley. A limo will whisk us there, we'll play croquet with a world-renown master, have champagne massages, and end the adventure with a candlelit dinner. Romantic, playful, a chance to get out together.

But no. Larry is stuck with "a dozen lawyers" at his Atherton estate. His former assistant-turned-girlfriend is suing him for sexual harassment. "Steve [Jobs] thinks I should change the Oracle voice mail system. 'Hello, thank you for calling Oracle. If you'd like to sue Larry, press 1. If you have friends or family who'd like to sue Larry, press 2. If your pet would like to sue Larry, press 3.'"

"You're taking this really well," I say.

"Oh sweetie," Larry coos, "I'm so sorry I can't make it. I'll call you tonight when all the lawyers are gone."

As I look back on this evening, the amazing thing is that while I was disappointed, I wasn't really hurt. I barely minded being blown off at all. Because Larry had called me "sweetie."

Larry's schedule was so crowded we ended up dating only semiannually, but it made me feel good. Having a powerful guy attracted to me was the only high I had in my personal life. There was only one little thing that bugged me. For all the dates we planned, he often canceled, and always at the last minute. Why did I put up with this? For the power? He called the shots, he had the influence, he saw me as optional. Wait a sec, *he* had the power . . . like, *all* of it.

I began to realize that what I cared for, what I needed, was to see myself reflected in a powerful man's shiny surface. Oh, to appear as that reflection! Over time I saw that reflection more clearly—a scared young woman, unsure, and anxious as she waited to mess up, to make a fashion faux pas, to be ditched, to be dumped. Such foolish reliance on false idols never builds one's own true value.

How do women date the rich and famous? How do they make sure they're always having a good hair day, their outfit is hot, their nails are impeccable, their face is clear and well made up, they have the right shoes and bag, they don't get nervous, they order the right thing, they can discuss whatever random topic is thrown their way? It was exhausting. I was done. I did, however, remember what Larry said about the Internet. A year later I started a company that provided Internet-based promotions, and it made me a few million.

Larry was introduced into my life as a diversion, but I learned some helpful lessons from him, particularly about dealing with public attack and perception. In the heat of a legal battle with his former trusted assistant and then lover (I cannot imagine what that felt like), he could enjoy Steve Jobs's suggested new voice mail message. It might have made him cringe inside, but he carried himself like an elegant Mandarin warlord. Mess with him and he'd certainly reciprocate, but he wouldn't show that his feathers had been ruffled. Likewise, when people lavished him with praise, he made light of it.

And the supreme self-confidence I found so seductive in all three billionaires? I finally admitted that I couldn't get it from osmosis . . . I'd have to develop it myself.

Why Borrow When You Can Build?

People do this with companies and job titles, too. They rely on the power and prestige of these external items to give them value. But they're borrowing power, not necessarily building it.

When you give your power to your company or your title, you define yourself by the work you do rather than your innate self-worth. If the job goes bye, so does your self-worth. I've been there. It's not pretty. Giving your power to an ideal, as when I decided to "become Bill Gates," isn't the worst power offense, but it's still borrowing—not summoning your power from within.

Are you borrowing power or building it? Here's how to tell: if you feel challenged, if you feel like you're growing, learning, and stretching each day, if you are acquiring new skills, trying to be the best *you* possible, you're building power. If you were to lose your job tomorrow, you know you'd find a new, better gig. You're not wasting time kissing up and playing office politics; you're investing time building your skill set.

I didn't become truly successful in business until I made the decision to stop giving away my right to feel powerful to a man or a title or even my company of the moment. *Power meant that supreme self-confidence I had seen in Bill so many years ago. Power meant I didn't have to grovel any longer, for I brought value to the table, too.* I've seen so many people date or borrow power instead of creating it for themselves. Maybe we don't know how, don't think we can, or we let ourselves get shut down by society or people in our workplace. But *this* is the quest—to find our own power and keep it and grow it. I did it through my career; others do it through raising their families or their role in the community. Either way, start where it feels easiest, and then expand your personal power to the other realms of your life.

It took me decades to find peace and power in my life. Whenever I got wobbly I'd get in trouble because I'd start looking for power outside instead of within. You've got to look inside alone. That's where you find yourself. And that kind of power no one can ever take away. Here are some ways to power up so that when you're in a bind, you'll be able to tough it out without getting wobbly.

POWERING UP

There will be challenging times when you want someone else to take care of you or your troubles. But these, my friends, are things one cannot delegate. If you "power up" ahead of time, you'll greatly increase your chances of not only surviving but thriving.

1. Think about that Bill Gates's sense of supreme confidence in his ability to design his and Microsoft's fu-

ture. Do you have that confidence? If so, in what areas of your life do you have it? If not, what would be the easiest areas in which to start developing it? Go for it.

2. Think about how Larry Ellison dealt with attack. He knew he'd emerge triumphant, and so he wasn't ruffled. He declared war, and then he calmly executed his strategy. How do you react when attacked or insulted? Do you lash out or keep your cool? If the former, what self-image, what illusion, could you conjure? Mongol warlord? Xena? Gandhi?

3. Need more examples? Read the story about shaking hands with the rich and famous in Chapter 6. There's a lot to learn from Barbara Walters, Hillary Clinton, Stephen Hawking, and others.

4. What are your internal assets? List what you uniquely bring to the table, what skills or abilities that you've noticed in yourself or have been acknowledged by others (such as perseverance, problem solving, and efficiency). What are you doing to further develop these skills and abilities? To develop additional ones?

5. What's your brand: what three adjectives describe you? Is this the brand you want? If so, what power does it convey? If not, pick your new brand and the power it will showcase.

(continues)

6. What's your creed: what beliefs and values do you live by? Is this the creed you want? If not, define your new one.

7. Do you like being you? Are you happy with who you are? If not, describe who you want to be. Get to know yourself. Meditate, pray, exercise—somehow get time alone daily to get to know yourself.

8. As you come to know yourself better, you'll reinforce your brand and live by your creed more consistently. Yes, it takes investment. But what could matter more?

COOL FREE RESOURCES

Go to www.RulesForRenegades.com and download "Overcoming Adversity," "Seeking Balance via Connection," "Power Boosters," "New Illusion Worksheet," and "Future Planning Worksheet," and see the Personal Development section, too.

Rock Rejection and Finesse Failure

Making Gallons of Tea in a Geisha Training Room . . . and a Seven-Figure Mistake

It's never the end of the world.
It's already tomorrow in Australia.

CHARLES M. SCHULZ

WHAT HOLDS US back from our dreams more than anything else? Fear of failure. So let's tackle it head on. Sooner or later you're going to fail. In fact, you may fail over and over. Afraid you'll make a wrong move and get your butt fired? Then take an easy job in some bureaucracy. If you want to be a successful entrepreneur or intrapreneur, you'll have to learn to embrace risk and grab for opportunity, even if sometimes you fail big.

Now ask yourself: What would you do if you were guaranteed to be a smashing success? Why not go for it? When you try to get something and it doesn't work out, you haven't lost anything. You didn't have it then, and you don't have it now. I don't want to be relentlessly upbeat, so let's cop to it: perhaps you feel you lost something in the process of taking a risk—time, effort, or money. These things can be "lost" in the short term, but in the long term you gained experience, knowledge, new contacts, and new ideas. I've found that every risk I've taken has resulted in a gain in the long term, even though I didn't always see it initially. You won't always measure up—I sure haven't—but that doesn't mean you have to walk away from the game. *You're playing to win, not to avoid losing.* You can always bounce back from any fail-ure. The key is to fail *forward*, where the pain of the failure is reduced by the benefit of the lessons it brings.

Flirting with Disaster

I'm the poster child for failure on an epic degree. Think you've messed up? Listen to these whoppers:

Ever been dumped and didn't know why? Ever had a job you hate? Ever had both at the same time? After Bill Gates dumps me, I reflect on my experience as a female. I'm a failure. I've never really figured out how to feel comfortable with my femininity. I finally bagged a powerful, famous guy, started to get emotionally attached, then blew it. Breathing the testos-terone-filled air at Microsoft couldn't be helping.

Flipping through *Vogue* magazine in my office at Microsoft, I am intoxicated by a photo of a geisha. Hey … maybe this is it … Femininity + power. A light goes off in my head. Beneath the layered silk and satin of the kimono, beneath the porcelain painted mask, nothing, nothing purrs feminine like the word *geisha.* My business mind loves it. Yeah, I'll be the first Ameri-can geisha in Japan. I'll storm the market. I'll *own* it. I'll start American Geisha, Incorporated, maybe even sell franchises, take the company public, make a zillion bucks. Then I'll rip off these golden handcuffs, march out the Microsoft door, and I won't look back.

This has got to be the most brilliant, original business idea ever; I can't *believe* no one else has thought of it. I scramble to find a teacher and begin my geisha training. My plan is to train by night, work at Microsoft by day.

. . .

In her tiny tearoom near Seattle's Japanese Garden, Mrs. Nakamora starts me out with some pinches, some particulars. She tugs at my jeans and T-shirt, trying to size me. She steps back, tilts her head, squints her eyes as she says, "The way of geisha, the Flower and Willow world, is for few. Years of training, at least five, in singing, dancing, playing *shamisen*, learning art of conversation," she's circling, looking me up and down. "You will wear very heavy uncomfortable kimono, very heavy uncomfortable wig, very thick uncomfortable makeup. And shoes . . . "

"Uncomfortable, right?"

"Right. You will speak Japanese. Every night entertain obnoxious drunk men, often till dawn."

Heck, I'm with obnoxious, sober men all day long. At least these drunk guys have an excuse. "Great. When do I start?"

"Next Tuesday, 6 p.m."

My training starts with posture and etiquette. Mrs. Nakamora wants me to master grace and poise, key to being a successful geisha—the Japanese word meaning "artist." I long to enter this exotic Flower and Willow world.

"Stand straight—shoulders back, not hunched like old lady."

"Chin in—not like turtle sticking head out of shell."

"Balance weight lightly—no flopping side to side like fish."

. . .

After two months of drifting weightlessly—with massive effort, I might add—about the teahouse Mrs. Nakamora says, "You done for now." I hope that's better than it sounds. I also hope she'll postpone my lessons on the *shamisen*, that Japanese banjo thingie. I never was good at stringed instruments.

I get lucky. Next we start *chado*, the meticulous Japanese tea ceremony. I do the lessons over and over. Sometimes I'm overeager, adding too much powdered tea to the water. Sometimes I'm distracted, letting the water boil too long. Sometimes the water is too hot; other times it's too cold. Often as I whisk, boiling green water splashes all over the low lacquer preparation table. Mrs. Nakamora hovers over me, closing her eyes in pained dismay.

"Again. Measure carefully, heat water until first small bubbles. Stop heat before boiling. Be patient."

"Again. Use whisk with less effort in wrist. Be graceful."

"Again. Pour slowly. Slow-ly. Do not spill. Be leisurely."

"Again. Pour seat of honor first. Be appropriate."

"Again. Kneel like lady, not cowboy. Be poised."

"Again. Balance. No falling on buttocks when pouring. Be ladylike."

"Again."

"Again."

"Again."

When I get it just right, I can sense it, smell it, as swirls of fresh-cut grass and hay mingle in a single thread of sexy steam that sways seductively up, up, up. Mrs. Nakamora is getting a taste of me, strong like her tea.

Even though I can train only one night per week with her, I have an engineer's focus on my lessons. I tell Mrs. Nakamora she'll get shares in American Geisha, Inc. She webs the fingers of her left hand over her mouth, laughs demurely, and reaches with her right for the cash to cover my class fee.

· · ·

A month later, Mrs. Nakamora tells me I've earned my geisha name. "I call you Ichisaku. It means first blossom, like first flowers of cherry blossom. Reminder that you first blossom, then become true geisha."

I'm grinding out code by day, gracing out geisha by night. One night an old friend of Mrs. Nakamora comes to town. This Mr. Nishi is a Japanese businessman, and Mrs. Nakamora wants me to run my ideas about American Geisha, Inc., by him.

"*Hajime mashite* [nice to meet you], Ichisaku-san," smiles Mr. Nishi.

"*Doo itashi mashite* [thank you], Nishi-san," I say, bowing low, for I am the caterpillar, the butterfly wannabe, grubbing, groveling at the bottom of this exotic food chain. But now, it is time for tea. I heat the water to the ideal temperature, whisk the powdered tea gently into it, and kneel to pour Nishi a cup. I rise, shuffle over to Nakamora, kneel and pour again. No spilling, no falling. I do better than I could have dreamed.

"You are most unique, Ichisaku," Nishi nods. "One day, when you are fully trained, perhaps I will introduce you to a patron. Since I already am one," he tips his eyes, "I will not offer myself."

"Thank you, Nishi-san. I am most honored that you have taken an interest in me." Did I just say that? Really? This I-am-most-honored-that-you-would-deign-to-find-me-the-least-bit-interesting stuff is hard to swallow, let alone say out loud without snorting into my kimono sleeve. Oh, to be a full geisha, when I won't have to say these things, do this sycophantic scraping.

After Nishi leaves. Nakamora turns to me, eyes shining with pride. "*Hai*," she puffs. "You have patron one day, Ichisaku. *Hai*."

"*Hai*," I sigh, sipping the intoxicating tea. She's given me a glorious glimpse into the Flower and Willow world and I want more, more, more. Yes, I will become a geisha. Yes, I will entertain powerful men. Yes, I will be wealthy, independent, untouchable. My life will overflow with beauty and art. I will be the butterfly, flitting from party to party, eager admirers at my wings, always wanting more, *always* unable to get it.

The next week Mrs. Nakamora says, "Much work, Ichisaku, much work to become geisha, to get patron, to build business."

"*Sumimasen* [excuse me], Nakamora-san. I know this is many years away, but will you please explain the role of the patron?"

"*Hai*, Ichisaku. After many months, if client finds geisha most pleasing, he offers to be patron. There is ceremony and geisha is bound to him, her patron."

"Bound? Like, tied?"

"No. Bound—she belongs to him in special way. She may entertain other clients, but not as she entertains patron."

"Entertains in a special way? How?"

"Geisha cannot sleep with other men. Only with patron."

"Sleep?! Like, have sex?"

"*Hai*. All geishas hope for patron. Geisha lifestyle veeeery costly. With patron geisha may build great fortune, own assets like home, stocks, bonds, for her retirement. Without patron, geisha bound to house that sponsors her."

"Do I understand correctly: a patron gives the geisha money, and she has sex with him?"

"Faaaar deeper relationship than that, Ichisaku, faaaar deeper."

"Okay, but—"

"But if you seek what Americans call 'bottom line,' then *hai*, you correct."

Correct. *Hai*. It's taken me four months of training Tuesday nights to learn that, if I launch and run American Geisha Inc., I'll essentially be a pimp. And if I'm a geisha myself, I'll be some-body's ho.

Why didn't she explain this to me during all that trial, all that tea? And why didn't *I* do my homework? No independ-ence. No powerful position. No flitting butterfly. An admirer, one not of my choosing, may attain me, *own* me. Ouch.

"Nakamora-san, you have been kind to me for the past four months. I feel foolish. I didn't know, didn't do enough research into the Flower and Willow world."

"What troubles you, Ichisaku? Patron's role?"

"Yes. I don't feel ... can't fulfill ... this patron thing. I just ... "

"Geishas very respected in Japan, Ichisaku. Here, in Amer-ica, Japanese customs, traditions, not always understood."

"I'm ... sorry." I reach forward, urge her out from the ki-mono, taking her tiny, soft hands in my large, hard ones. Her eyes open wide. My intimacy, my inappropriate touch, startles her. "*Domo* [thanks], Nakamora-san. *Domo arigato gozaimasu* [thank you so very much]."

Nakamora-san just stares. I hold her hands, squeeze, re-lease. Then bow, turn, slowly walk away. I don't look back.

The caterpillar crawls away. Away from the Flower and Wil-low world, away from this potential megamillion-dollar empire, away from this fantasy of feminine power. Back to my box, back to my bottom line.

Failing Forward

Unhappy as I was with this adventure, I did go back to my bottom line. I decided that instead of concentrating on what I'd done wrong, I would concentrate on what I was going to do right next time.

The first thing I'd learned was: do something, but do nothing important. To rock rejection and finesse failure it helps to take a time out. Retreat after a whopping rejection or failure to retrench, to regain your strength and clarity. Had I done that after the Bill bust, the American Geisha adventure would have been bypassed. But I had let Bill's rejection get the better of me, and I followed it up with an encore. Had I taken a time-out, I would have realized that letting myself heal and have some low-profile time before diving into another project would have been better for me. It's like a rebound relationship: starting another relationship after an icky breakup rarely eases the pain. It simply postpones and often multiplies it.

What if you're obsessing, dwelling on your failure, and you're feeling superstuck? Then you can do two things. First, start something positive. Embrace a fresh hobby, take a class in a fascinating or fun topic, or do some volunteer work. These are all great ways to rebuild confidence without taking a whopping emotional risk. Even an hour or two per week of a new activity will bring upbeat energy into your life and remind you of your many talents. Look into local colleges or nonprofits where you can try something new without making a major time commitment.

Another useful activity is to list what's great about you. Yes, it sounds hokey. Over coffee or even e-mail, solicit input from others as to your fabulous qualities.

After you ask a few people, you'll see considerable overlap in their replies. Post your positive qualities on your bathroom mirror. Put a list in your wallet, too. Read it at least twice per day. Understanding your great qualities helps you identify what you might want to do next.

The second thing I learned is that I'd failed *at* something—but *I* wasn't a failure. In fact, I had actually become more successful at some things. Even though I picked an inappropriate business to start, at least I got my mojo together and got something rolling (instead of wallowing in self-pity). The geisha experience boosted my confidence in my selling skills. Heck, if I could sell Nakamora and Nishi on my geisha potential, wasn't the sky the limit? What else could I sell? How else could I define myself? Maybe I had learned to embody Bill Gates's supreme confidence after all.

Maybe most important, I'd learned to separate my personal needs from a business aspiration. I wanted to start American Geisha not out of a desire to build a company but out of a desire to fix myself—to figure out how to become female *and invulnerable*—and as a way to run away from my situation. A company can't fix you or your life. Yes, starting a company or working within one certainly provides terrific opportunities for personal development, but attaching a personal goal to the launching of a company was a bad idea. My particular goal couldn't be fast-tracked through commerce; rather, it required self-reflection and more life experience to achieve it. Finally, I'd learned to do my homework before getting too deeply involved in a project.

And of course, I could make a killer cup of tea.

The forward speed of my failure started to pick up momentum. I'd learned to separate business from myself, I'd sold some people on my potential, I'd gained some confidence. And I'd decided to forget about dating Bill Gates—I'd *become* him. I had made *something* happen, even if it wasn't what I'd set out to do. Using the American Geisha experience as a springboard, I dove into the deep end of the business pool: selling high-end services to the Fortune 1000 through my new company, Corporate Computing International. When CCI competed with the Big Six accounting firms I wasn't as intimidated as I might have been had the geisha experience not occurred. Using what I had learned from American Geisha, I started the *right* company, and sold a rare product to a high-end customer base I had little experience with. I had *failed forward*.

CCI was a great success for two years. Then came December 1994.

The first page of the article in *Wired* magazine rolls off my fax. As I read it, my knees buckle and I fall to the floor. It's an exposé about my meditation teacher Rama (whom you'll read more about in Chapter 7) and his "evil cult" that "commits business fraud." What are they talking about? I read on. Ohmygod—a few paragraphs in, I'm mentioned as a key follower. It sounds as if everyone who studies with him is a brainwashed agent of corporate destruction—and I'm a ringleader. Hey, I have 700 of the Fortune 1000 as clients! Getting them has nearly killed me, working 80 to 90 hours per week, living on airplanes and in hotels. I'm literally shaking as the article ends. I only see Rama a few times a year now. I'm not sure what is and isn't true about him, but one thing is crystal clear: both my reputation and my company are toast.

This man is the father figure who taught me how to meditate, encouraged my spiritual path, and sheltered me in his ashram when I was a foundering youngster. I've always considered him a force for good; I was happy to sign the contract turning half of CCI over to him, especially since I'd get a free sales force of his students in exchange. And the profits could go to starting up new meditation centers.

Sure, Rama and I have had our challenges. I've repeatedly suggested he charge less for his teaching, ask less from the tithing monks, allow everyone to acquire some assets for their old age. Sure, he kicked me out of the ashram for being insubordinate. But I didn't stay away for long. He meant home to me, however weird it was.

I call Rama for support, and he pressures me to give him 10 percent more of CCI. I tell him that the 50 percent of my company he already owns is generous enough. Then he sics his lawyers on me, and the threatening begins. When did this all get so screwed up? A spiritual teacher threatening his student for more money? I'm as likely to cave in to his attack dogs as I am to climb the Himalayas without oxygen. It's all become so clear: Rama isn't who he used to be. I need to get out of this gig. The next time he calls me, I say, "Please take your 50 percent, and let's part company." He threatens me again. So I add, "Or I'll tank the business just to be free of you."

If you think I was an innocent victim, let me clarify. First, my gut had sounded the alarm, saying things were getting a little strange in Rama's world, but I had chosen to ignore it. Like about a zillion times. I met him when I was 17, he was my surrogate dad, how could I now dis him? Second, I ignored—okay, denied—that things were messed up because I didn't want to admit that Rama was a master of emotional manipulation. The pattern went like this: I'd question something sensitive, usually a financial matter. He'd say I wasn't spiritually evolved enough to understand, then I'd cave to my inner critic who was shrieking, "See? I *told* you not to question him!" and I'd retreat and beat myself up for a few hundred hours. The older and more confident I became, the more I'd push a little further, play Columbo, and scratch my head and say I really didn't get it. Then he'd push back even harder. My first mistake was to cave in to authority, allowing myself to be pushed around. My second mistake was to skip saying "Whoa! This ain't no spiritual sanctuary!" and head for the nearest ashram exit.

Four key CCI staffers suddenly quit "for no reason." Business falls off steeply. I'm spending my days doing constant damage control. The focus of 1995 becomes trying to sell the company, which is going down fast. I decide to sue *Wired* for libel, kicking off an emotionally draining two years.

I end up having to sell CCI for a third of its value. I lose about $8 million on the transaction, and have to build up my business and my reputation from scratch—all because I forfeited my sense of myself as a leader to be Rama's follower, because I chose power by association instead of building it myself. To top it off, my sense of self-worth is precisely calibrated to my company, so now I have none until I start another business. But wait, there's more! *Wired* and I settle out of court and I can't even celebrate; the *San Francisco Chronicle* prints *Wired*'s press release claiming they won the case! (At least after that debacle, *Wired* now has a fact-checking department.) The *Wired* article was right about one thing: Rama has a lot more mansions and exotic cars than I knew about. I never talk to him again. Years later he commits suicide.

Part of me wishes I didn't learn all the best life lessons the hard way—though I wouldn't swear that these were worth $8 million and several years of my life—but there are some crucial take-homes here. Listen to your gut. Then act on it. A large part of success in life involves this.

Next, extract the lesson that shows you how to fail forward. With the *Wired* incident it became crystal clear to me that it was time to finally take full charge of my life, and that when I followed someone else's lead, I screwed up. I had to develop compassion for myself, too. I saw myself as a together, professional woman, hardly a pushover. How had I been so thoroughly snagged in Rama's trap? This line of questioning led to beating myself up, which achieved nothing. So I had to cut myself some slack, had to suck it up, deal with my business and staff, soothe our customers, and keep it together. In time I activated my fighting spirit (see the tips on dealing with adversity, pp.122–123) and I finally understood, at the deepest level of my being, that no matter what comes my way I will emerge triumphant. Maybe I'll be a bit bruised and worse for the wear, but I'll get through it. Knowing that fact considerably reduced the level of fear I was willing to tolerate in my life going forward. Now when I think "What's the worst that could happen?" nothing even comes close to what I've already been through! The Rama experience with the *Wired* finale worked wonders to build inner strength. That's how I failed forward in this case.

An even bigger benefit from this hellacious experience was that I finally learned to ask for help. This attack was too huge, too intense, too devastating to handle alone. I had to shed my Lone Ranger mask and admit I needed a shoulder to lean on. I was 32 years old and had finally allowed myself to reach out to others.

Remember that rejection and failure feel personal, but you have a choice as to whether you take it that way. An emotional reaction can result in a questionable business decision (like a lawsuit), which more often than not will be a huge waste of time, energy, and money. Separately, if you're simply being authentic and you're targeted for bad publicity, it's probably either because you're high profile or because something you did or said threatened someone. We all have the option to choose a low-profile life. But if you want to make a difference in the world, you're probably going to upset some people along the way. So stand tall.

Unless you change the present, the past will predict the future. Until you change your state of mind, you'll repeat the mistakes of your past. When you're stuck, ask yourself: How can I bounce back higher and harder? After I read the *Wired* article, I curled into a ball of self-pity for about 12 hours. Sure, I had some hard days after that when I wondered if this horror show would ever end. But I knew I had to rise above the pettiness of this public attack, dust myself off, and go out there guns a-blazin'. It's a decision you make alone, in the dark, in the quiet; you choose to find the upside of the agony.

You Suck! You're Super!

Remember how I said that everything is an illusion? Think of this story when people either speak unkindly of or to you—and also when they sing your praises.

There once was a monk who lived in a tiny hut on a hill overlooking a village. He kept to himself, only coming down to the village for food. In that village a young woman had become visibly pregnant, and when her screaming father insisted on knowing who her lover was, she named the monk. An angry mob marched up the hill and stormed the monk's hut.

"You are a disgrace to Buddhism!" they shouted. "All these years we've given you alms and now you impregnate one of our women! You should be ashamed! How dare you call yourself a holy man!"

"Is that so?" the monk said, and returned to his meditation.

Time passed, and the child was born. The young woman's father again marched up the hill and handed the baby to the monk. "Here. You take care of your bastard child. You caused this problem, you live with the consequences."

"Is that so?" The monk said. He accepted the child and returned to his meditation.

After a few weeks the young woman was overcome with remorse for falsely fingering the monk. She told her father that the monk was not her lover after all, that her true lover had left, and she wanted to raise the child on her own. Again her father marched up the hill, this time with the townspeople in tow.

"Please forgive our mistake. We are so sorry. What a truly holy man you are for tolerating our cruel words and caring for this child. We will relieve you now of this burden. The Buddha himself is singing your praises in the higher worlds, all the higher beings are smiling down on you, no greater monk has ever lived."

"Is that so?" The monk said, and returned to his meditation.

The moral of this story isn't "Do nothing and everything will work out okay." Nope. It's "Don't get bent out of shape when people dis you and don't get puffed with pride when people praise you." Neither changes your intrinsic value.

Four years after the article, and once the original *Wired* management team had been replaced by seasoned professionals, I asked some of the guys there what the point of the whole Rama article was. They looked at me, smiling, and said, "That issue sold a load of copies, Christine." Ohhhh. It was all about selling magazines. Duh! Silly me. Sheesh. I paused and remembered my friend Barry's favorite quote from the unnamed Russian hit man: "Is not personal. Is just business." Sometimes, my friends, you just have to let stuff roll off you. If people sling mud, shrug it off. If you sit still, it'll stick to you.

In the late 1990s the new staff of *Wired* wrote about me glowingly when I started my first venture capital fund, Artemis Ventures. In 2005, they recommended me as an on-air expert to CNN. Thanks, *Wired*. I think we finessed that failure.

Fall Down Seven Times, Get Up Eight

Failure seems to come in two flavors. The first is created internally: you didn't do enough research, you made a bad decision (my geisha experience), or you sabotaged yourself, and you let someone psych you out (my Rama experience). The second type of failure hits you from the outside. You've done all you could—practiced the Law of Attraction, focused on a positive outcome, worked your butt off, paid your dues, but the world didn't cooperate. Or maybe it was just your time to learn to deal with adversity. With this second type of failure, ask yourself if you gave it your best shot. If so, let it go; if not, resolve to give it your all next time. This attitude is balm to the sting of defeat.

A few years back I met a promising start-up team with a potentially fabulous future. Together we raised several million dollars of venture capital financing, built up a solid team, and ramped up sales. The company was on track for profitability in six months or so. Then, on the cusp of their success, the Internet bubble burst. Financiers got paranoid and stopped writing checks. The company was rapidly running out of money. Two of seven board members wanted to fund the company to profitability, but they couldn't carry the burden themselves. The majority of the existing financiers threw in the towel, and after a frenzied search for financing alternatives, the company shut their doors. The CEO sold the assets and the staff moved on.

The executive team got together and reviewed what they had learned from the experience. They now knew what roles they enjoyed most, they understood complex financing structures, they had learned about channel sales, and most of all, they had learned what it means to be entrepreneurs. Today the team members are involved in a number of exciting endeavors. Some have formed new businesses, others are intrapreneurs within large corporations, a few are trying out academia. In all their roles, they're running projects as if they have no certainty of additional outside financing. They have learned to become self-reliant and to let their new companies grow more organically, avoiding the high-risk rocketing pace of a venture-backed start-up.

Sometimes you may be stung so badly by a failure or rejection it takes time before you can stretch your swollen hand and grab the balm of a positive attitude. In this case, you'll want to work on desensitizing yourself. And the best way I've found is a Rejection Party. (See How to Throw a Rejection Party at the end of this chapter.)

Be Cool When You're Rejected

Rejection, unlike failure, comes in only one flavor: the external kind. This is when others just don't want to play with you. I've been rejected by potential hires ("I don't want this stinkin' job"), staff members who quit or weren't right for their role (more on this in Chapter 7), sales prospects (zillions of these) who wouldn't buy what I was selling, men who didn't want to date me, friends who decided I wasn't cool enough, you name it. When they say "No," I say "Next!" Remember the Rock Rejection Mantra:

> Some will.
> Some won't.
> So what?
> Someone's waiting.

Somebody out there wants what you have. Keep looking, keep asking, keep the faith, and focus on finding this person. I repeated the Rock Rejection Mantra many times when my agent was pitching my first book—which was rejected unanimously by 22 publishers. So I re-shaped it into a different book, the one that you're now reading. After 17 more rejections we sold this book—with several editors interested. It sold once I decided, deep inside myself, that regardless of 39 rejections, this book was going to happen—even if I had to print it myself. I dropped the fear of rejection and focused on attracting a kick-ass editor, someone who really "got" what my book was about.

A while back I was asked to speak at a retreat for a somewhat traumatized team. They were the key achievers in a consumer products company, and the competition had been hammering them steadily for several quarters. The top brass had decided that their team needed to be more entrepreneurial, so my job was to come in and encourage them to take risks, be accountable, and innovate more intensely. I had a series of phone calls with executive management and thought I understood the lay of the land, but I sent my presentation to the event planner in advance just to be sure.

During my presentation, I scanned the audience and saw two distinct reactions. The first were the smiling, nodding executives. The second were the scowling, defensive team members. The audience was polite enough during my presentation, but a handful of the evaluations afterward were scathing—loaded with personal insults and shocking in their hostility. It was clear afterward that these folks had no desire to increase risk taking, accountability, or innovation. Executive management had tossed me into a den of hostile, demoralized people and expected me to work a miracle.

After reading the evaluations I gave myself a whopping pep talk. Starting with:

Q-TIP: Quit Taking It Personally

Lesson learned. Now I always ask to talk to a few of the team members before going into a tricky turnaround.

It's essential to hear their side of the story. As a result, I've been able to turn hostile or threatened crowds into enthusiastic (or at least receptive) intrapreneurs.

You're going to experience adversity in life, and a lot of it if you take risks. Here's what I do to stay on track:

- Remember, it's all an illusion. Failure has rewards; success has dangers. Learn from both, and move on.

- Recall the vision that got you going. Spend a day working on your dream board. Don't do anything else; just let that dream get back on its feet.

- Practice the Law of Attraction: think about the things that will get you back on your feet, the people who will help you get up and running, the places you can go that will take you forward. Watch the movie *The Secret* again.

- If people tell you, "You can't" or "That's a lousy idea," congratulations; that usually means you're on to something.

- Sometimes you have to look the part, so do it and don't complain about it. If necessary, change your look to get the respect you deserve, as I did to build a customer base of the Fortune 1000.

- On the really dark days remember that you're still alive, you still can make a difference in your life, your community, and the world at large. This round may be over, but the game ain't over yet. Something great could happen tomorrow.

- At the risk of ticking off everyone ever held ransom by a telemarketer, consider that every "no" actually means "maybe"—either you need to pitch in a more compelling way (explain their return on investment, success statistics, how you'll help them crush their competitors) *or* you don't have what the prospective customer needs yet.

- Take 100 percent responsibility for your life—you are no one's victim. This means no blaming, no complaining, no trying to change others!

- When you're stuck or psyched out after a failure, help others. Do some volunteer work. It'll help you stop dwelling on negativity and will foster hope.

- Make and post a list of your awesome qualities. I still do this today. It's crucial to learn to boost your confidence and self-esteem.

Visualize the things you want coming into your life. I like to imagine that all my goals have already been achieved on the nonphysical level. It's my job to welcome them down to the physical realm. You can host many rejection parties, you can desensitize yourself to criticism, and still, every now and then you'll fail. This is yet another reason why it's great to have a mastermind group or an accountability partner or fabulous friends. We all need to vent or brainstorm when we fail, and having a prefab failure or rejection recovery group works wonders. With practice you'll learn to fail *forward* more often than not. You'll learn to rock rejection and finesse failure.

HOW TO THROW A REJECTION PARTY

It's one thing for me to tell you not to take rejection personally; it's another to pull it off. The key is to desensitize. Playwright Jean Kerr, author of *Please Don't Eat the Daisies*, used to clip out the most cutting words from newspaper critics' reviews of her plays and paste them onto her bathroom mirror. After looking at them day after day while brushing her teeth, she eventually stopped feeling offended by them. If this method works for you, terrific. My preferred method of desensitization is to throw a Rejection Party.

The Rejection Party: Type A

Gather ten or more people together (more is better). They can be colleagues, friends, members of a networking or mastermind group, or even strangers with a desire to learn.

Here are the rules:

1. Each person in the group forms a question for something they want, such as "Will you invest $100,000 in my new company?" or "Will you buy my widget?"

2. Now walk around the room, approaching the other participants one-on-one and asking them your question. They'll give you a "yes" or "no" answer, and will ask you their question too. You must give a "yes" or "no" answer. See step 3 for the rules on answering.

3. Keep a silent tally of the number of requests made of you. You can only answer "yes" if the person addressing you is making the tenth request. Say "no" to all others. Once you've said "yes," start counting again and say "no" to the next nine requests. You can say "no" however you want—apologetically, curtly, kindly— it's up to you. The goal is to simulate real-world rejection in order to become immune to it.

After repeatedly getting rejected, you'll find it doesn't hurt so badly. You come to realize that each rejection gets you closer to acceptance. Remember the Rock Rejection Mantra:

Some will.
Some won't.
So what?
Someone's waiting.

Keep asking and eventually you'll get a "yes."
Thanks to Jack Canfield for teaching me this technique.

(continues)

The Rejection Party: Type B

As much as I like Rejection Party Type A, I extended it to this new version, which I find mirrors the world more realistically. The requester must ask for the same thing, but can change his or her pitch, trying different approaches. For instance, the requester could say "Will you invest $100,000 in my new marketing company?" and the next time he or she could say, "Will you loan $100,000 to my new marketing company at 6 percent interest and a 10-year payback period?" The requestee is allowed to say "yes" if he or she finds the request compelling enough. He or she doesn't actually have to follow through (that is, fork over that $100,000) but must honestly be intrigued by the request.

COOL FREE RESOURCES

Go to www.RulesForRenegades.com and download "Mind Map Template," "Overcoming Adversity," "Goal Setting Worksheet," "New Illusion Design Worksheet," and "Future Planning Worksheet," and see the Personal Development section, too.

Learn to Love Networking

*Making Friends and Influencing
People in Unusual Ways at the
Clinton White House*

Call it a clan, call it a network, call it a tribe,
call it a family: whatever you call it, whoever
you are, you need one.

JANE HOWARD

Do you love to network? I do now, but I didn't always. I first learned about the value of networking on the set of the comedy sitcom *Laugh-In*, in the 1970s, when my elementary school class toured its Burbank studio and watched a taping of the show.

Goldie Hawn is dancing around the set in a pink and yellow daisy-patterned bikini. She weaves between four enormous black cameras on wheeled platforms. She passes Arte Johnson in an army costume, Lily Tomlin dressed as the "one ringy dingy" telephone operator, and a dozen guys in bell bottoms and big lapels. She dances under the lights; she dances in the dark places. Everyone is either talking or shouting across the stage to one another, women with clipboards run behind men walking really fast. Everyone is smiling, laughing, and having fun. And this is their *job*.

"You are soooo lucky," I whisper to Steve Snyder, whose dad had arranged this field trip.

"Yeah. I get to come here all the time," Steve says.

"So, how did your dad get this job?"

"He says he knows the right people."

I'm not sure what this means, but I decide then and there to make sure I know the right people so I can get a groovy job too. But how do I meet the right people? Later that evening I ask. "Dad, Steve Snyder's dad works on the set of *Laugh-In*. It's a great job. Steve said he got it because he knows the right people."

"I'll bet he does, Tiger Baby."

"How do I do that—know the right people?"

"Schmoozing. Talking with people. Charming them. Asking them to help you."

Emotional Equity Is More Valuable

I added the first name to my Rolodex when I was 19: Joel Kovner, the CEO of the bank where I worked. Today my Rolodex has more than 5,000 names, and through those people I know over a million more. Those 5,000 are friends and colleagues I treasure—the well I go to when I need advice, a sounding board, an introduction, or someone to slap me upside the head before I make a bad business mistake. Of those 5,000 people, there are probably 500 or so who would offer me whatever help I requested. It took me a while, but now I understand why.

Lots of people have a hard time asking for what they want; they don't want to be pests or they think they don't deserve it. So flip it around. *Don't think in terms of connecting with people to get what you want; think about how you can help them.*

Everyone thinks about financial equity, but building *emotional* equity is so much more valuable and satisfying. The more you help people get what they want, the more they'll help you. When you're networking, you're not just looking blindly for people who can give you stuff: you're looking to create another kind of family—people you care about, people who will care about you. Follow your intuition; it'll tell you whom to approach and how. Look for people to connect to, to develop relationships with. In the end, it's those relationships that matter, that will make the journey worthwhile.

Don't approach others with an open hand—that "lean and hungry look" oozes desperation. Have you ever noticed there's a physicality to the gimme? There's a way people look at you when they want something: eager, impatient, and expectant. Sometimes they are leaning forward, as if preparing to grab. They're watching for their moment, and if they don't get it, disappointment is reflected all over their faces. Relax, kick back in your mind, and just try to get to know the people you're talking to. Ask them about their businesses, their ideal customers, and their goals. Ask what they do for fun, find out what they care about. People have fascinating lives, businesses, challenges, and triumphs. Seek out these stories, and you'll gain valuable insights and maybe even lessons.

When I was in my thirties I used to think, "I do so many favors for Suzie-Q, but whenever I ask her, she doesn't help." I'd feel bitter or resentful: a closed fist instead of an open hand. Now I realize that there are larger laws of the universe at work. When people ask you for favors, do them if you can. Do them if you have the resources, the time, and the ability. Know that you'll get favors in return; just don't stress out if they don't come from people you've helped. I'm not advocating letting yourself be taken advantage of—you need to establish your own healthy boundaries. Putting your efforts out there gets the ball rolling; trust that the good will come back to you. Strapped for cash? That's often the very moment you should help someone else out with a loan or gift. Trust that *the universe has a perfect accounting system.*

Make Deposits in Your Karmic Bank Account

When you put out good energy it's like making deposits into your karmic bank account. Yes, you're helping people and doing good because it's fun and feels great—you're giving to give, not to get. But what happens as a result is that people often will show up out of the blue who want to help you. The reason to network is so that you can put yourself out there to meet those people

You already have friends in high places; you just might not know them yet. If you want to promote yourself and tell people what you're doing, start by asking them what they're doing, help them out, and get the good energy moving. Regardless of where you are in your career, networking is key. I write letters to public figures, I go see whoever is currently on the speaking circuit. As a result I've met and sought advice from Steve Jobs, Patch Adams, Jane Fonda, Erica Jong, Amy Tan, Andy Grove, and many more. I wanted to hear their stories, absorb their wisdom, and see if there was even a little thing that a nobody like me could do for a somebody like them. In the process I found some exceptional mentors. Find the people you want to meet and go hear them speak. Ask them questions; listen to their stories before you tell them yours.

Amazing things come into the lives of those who help others. A friend of mine loves to do political fund-raising. He also gives a ton of money to nonprofits in the areas of education and health. He believes that if we support the political candidates we care about, then we're more likely to get legislation passed to support the nonprofits. He works all day at his company and does fund-raising almost every night of the week. He's the hardest working nonpaid fund-raiser I know. And people just show up to help his business and his charitable causes left and right. He needs a celebrity to fly to Africa to promote AIDS care. In one or two phone calls it's done.

In the late 1990s, I volunteered with TechNet, a group of bipartisan technology executives who wanted to help the government connect more with Silicon Valley. It wasn't really about pushing our initiatives forward but about bringing technology into the government to increase efficiency. The idea of my tax dollars actually working and not being spent on excessive bureaucracy fascinated me.

Well, I was invited not only to go to the White House on several occasions, some of them social, but also to work with Al Gore's National Performance Review. Gore's goal was to create a government that worked better and cost less. I was asked to help develop the Clinton administration's Intranet strategy, and then to help motivate all the government agencies to get an Intranet site up within 90 days. It was a thrill. I had the good fortune to work (unpaid) with courageous and committed people like the late great Greg Woods, an executive from the private sector hand-picked by Gore to help tune up government technology.

Also in the late 1990s, I met Cindy and Greg Shove, a couple who were launching Impact Online, today known as VolunteerMatch (www.volunteermatch.org). Their vision was to help Americans learn about non-profit causes and opportunities for volunteer work. The business leapt to the next level when Jay Backstrand, an executive from Sun Microsystems, took the helm as executive director at VolunteerMatch. In time I introduced Jay to Greg Woods. Before I knew it, VolunteerMatch was invited to the White House, Clinton endorsed it, and today more than 3 million people have been "matched" with volunteer opportunities. On September 11, 2001, when the Red Cross Web site was overloaded with offers of help, VolunteerMatch swooped in and provided a redundant Web site.

And, of course, my up-down, on-again off-again acquaintance with Bill Gates started when I asked for money for AIDS. Over time we established rapport and kept in touch via e-mail. Today it delights me to see how strong Bill's support of AIDS-related causes is.

One last example: offering to help a friend with a struggling start-up resulted in an introduction to an angel investor, which led to an invitation to invest in an angel group, which resulted in getting to invest in Google in its early days and enjoying a fabulous financial gain.

The biggest benefit of all these networking experiences was a radical perspective change. *With each experience, I better understood how aspects of the world worked, resulting in my ability to effect change and, ultimately, my realization that I really can do anything.* I just need to find the person who can help me achieve a specific goal. Frequently it's someone who has a goal I can help support, and we will provide encouragement or opportunity for each other. Helping others get what they want is both a path to connection as well as career growth. And it is fun, too.

Networking isn't just a way to find help or money; it's a way to build your tribe. I was a loner for the first three decades of my life. I decided at age seven, when my two best friends died a few months apart, that maybe being close to people wasn't such a great idea. So I always stayed safely distant. Oh, I had friends, but I didn't let anyone get in very deep. There was a wall inside me that people couldn't get past. The only "person" I relied on was God, my own personal version, who was my best pal and the one I talked with when I was scared or lonely.

I didn't feel deeply connected to my career in the software industry until I started writing a weekly column and giving speeches on a regular basis. These two activities enabled me to interact more deeply with people, to answer their questions, to try to understand their problems, and to offer a little help. Forming these connections helped me to feel part of something bigger in my working world.

By daring to listen, to help, to invite people into my life, they have invited me into theirs. Networking is marketing. Marketing yourself, marketing your uniqueness, marketing what you want to stand for. The better you market yourself, the more likely you are to be in high demand and to be top-of-mind when someone has an opportunity to offer. The result is you'll be well positioned to give and receive potentially great things.

Schmoozing for Fun, Profit, and . . .

The business world is a meritocracy: if you've got the talent and the ambition, you're going to find a way to make things work. Likewise, if you're an intrapreneur and continuously demonstrate entrepreneurial behavior, you'll shine within your corporation. In 1995 I formed Digital Dames, a network of more than 30 female CEOs, founders, intrapreneurs, and senior executives in the high-tech world. The goal was to help empower female entrepreneurs in Silicon Valley. We met once a quarter to give one another advice and encouragement.

This wasn't a hen party, where we chitchatted about the best place to buy cute shoes. (Okay, the topic of shoes did come up every now and then.) We were there to get advice on how to improve a marketing campaign or rustle up more capital or to cheer when a member got her company funded, made an essential business contact, or saw her stock soar. The positive energy at those meetings was palpable; we always left feeling inspired and supported.

Leveraging on the success of Digital Dames my friend Mark Tebbe and I founded Schmoozefest in 1996 to bring together people from tech, venture capital, media, accounting, legal, and more. Having recently returned to the San Francisco Bay Area, this seemed like a smart way to reconnect with old friends and make new ones. Schmoozefest was at my house, and the rules were simple: it was by invitation only (we'd invite 400, get about 120 to 200 each time); no shoes were allowed, and everybody had to bring drinks, entrées, or desserts. Costumes were highly encouraged. Only names were permitted on the name tags—no companies or titles; we wanted people to talk to one another regardless of "rank." Every party—we gave 15 of them over four years —had a theme: Çinco de Mayo, Tropical Paradise (for months after that one, I was sweeping up the sand I had trucked in), Chinese New Year (with customized messages in the fortune cookies that promised fame, fortune, and funding), *The Godfather*, Mardi Gras, Caveman Days (with lots of fur and dirt-smeared bare midriffs that night), and more.

I'm not sure what people loved most about them. Was it the chance to be fanned by man-slaves when they arrived at the Cleopatra's Love Den bash? Was it the tar pit at the Caveman party, full of old computers and electronics? Or maybe the thousands of dollars' worth of wine brought in by the high bidders from the Napa Valley Wine Auction? Regardless, everyone enjoyed the sight of a man who managed billions padding around in Tweety Bird slippers and a key male angel investor dressed in drag with *way* too much blue eye shadow on. Everyone cut loose in this themed and costumed world. And roughly $50 million worth of deals were done at each party.

One of the best parts for me was the pride people had in their contributions. A major TV anchor brought chocolate-dipped strawberries once. He stood by them most of the night, explaining how to get the chocolate to the exact right consistency so it would form a thick coat on each strawberry. More men than women pushed the catering staff aside and took over the kitchen.

Schmoozefest was featured in a ton of media coverage, but that was the icing on the cake. Through Schmoozefest I was reacquainted with mover and shaker Dan Lynch, who promptly introduced me to Joan Ziegler, who then told Chris Lynch and me about each other. She thought we'd be a perfect pair. Chris and I were so busy that despite Joan's best efforts we didn't manage to hook up. Six months passed. I met a publicist at a networking event, she pitched me to *Fortune* magazine; they featured me in an article with a provocative photo. Chris saw it, he called me (finally!), we went out on a date, and two years later we were married. No online dating service, no personal ad, just networking, making friends, and helping one another out. I am now convinced of this:

> Life = the people you meet + what you create together

It's easy to get carried away by the heady feeling of having a profile in a magazine, a favorable mention of your company, or a microphone stuck under your nose. But remember: the media aren't there to serve you; you're there to be of service, too. How can you be a connector? Can you put journalists in touch with helpful sources? Can you help others get their products and services featured? Where is an information gap that you can plug? I got my gig writing a column for *PC Week* because a wonderful mentor, Jesse Berst, introduced me to the top brass at the magazine. We talked about how I might be the person who could demystify new technology for large corporations. Then I brought bouquets, not demands, to the table. I wrote five sample columns for free to show them how I might be of service to their readers. After I got the job, I read every bit of reader mail (sometimes I'd get hundreds of letters and e-mails a month) and did my best to respond to their questions and concerns.

Shaking Hands with the Rich and Infamous

How you respond and how you interact with people speaks volumes about both you and them. The handshake is my favorite method of nonverbal information gathering. Have you ever noticed that handshakes speak their own secret language? If you pay attention you'll hear them whisper, yell, fret, or fawn. And handshakes of the rich and famous—they're amplified, ranging from sirens wailing to the Beatles singing "I Wanna Hold Your Hand." I learned this at a high-profile party.

I'm at a soirée in New York when I meet the handshake on the far end of the spectrum. The band plays "Getting to Know You" as I receive an obligatory up-down jerk from junk bond king Michael Milken. Avoiding eye contact, Michael looks over my shoulder, searching for someone with status. "Isn't There Someone More Interesting Here?" his handshake grumbles.

My favorite is the I'm Sincerely Pleased to Meet You and I Mean It shake, a double grip sporting three up-down pumps, meaningful eye contact, and a personal comment. For a fleeting moment, the shakee feels like the belle of the ball. If I'm ever a VIP, this is the shake I'll master. My first encounter with the Sincere shake is at the White House, when I meet Hillary Clinton. She's all warmth and compliments, asking about my experience as a woman in the early days of Microsoft. There's a smallish crowd here, so I figure she was briefed on the guests she didn't know. Extensive background checks are required to get this close to the First Lady—the First Lady who memorized information on me. I am enthralled. Now she asks my opinion of contemporary poets.

.   .   .

I meet the Sincere shake again at a swanky Manhattan watering hole, where my friend Joel is celebrating his daughter's debut at Carnegie Hall. I mingle with the glamorous crowd, feeling a little self-conscious as my jewels are not precious, my gown not couture. Barbara Walters is in the corner. She's smaller than I'd expected—tiny, feisty, like an action figure. I introduce myself and she looks up smiling. I believe she is sincerely pleased to meet me and she means it.

"I love *The View*. It's a wonderful show," I gush. We are still holding hands.

"Thank you so much for saying that. Lately more people mention *The View* than *20-20*. Why, do you think?"

"Because we want to drink coffee and chat with our girlfriends, like you do on the show—"

"And none of us have time to in our real lives—"

"Yes."

"We need to change that," she says with a brisk nod.

And I want to, to have time for girlfriends, but I am too busy trying to become a *player*, and I want her to be my friend, and I want to call her "Babs" and have some girl talk right here, right in the middle of this fancy private dining room where everyone except Barbara looks like they don't want to know me because I'm not red-carpet perfect so I clearly am not a player. But I don't cozy up to Barbara, because it doesn't feel right. It feels kinda kiss ass.

A woman cozies up to *me*, though, and it's clear she's feeling a little insecure, too. Her ex-husband is in Switzerland evading the IRS. Everyone knows this, it's all over the news, and to top it off she's a major fund-raiser for President Clinton, so it's especially awkward. She offers me the Oh, I Don't Care shake — it's a limp one, with a soggy lifeless hand grasp, and no hearty up-down pumps. I easily slide my hand free. Shaking isn't what she wants anyway. She wants to meet single men in Manhattan; might I know any? Yes, she doesn't want a handshake at all; she wants a booty call.

· · ·

The second time I shake with Hillary we're in the garden of a private Los Altos home. Once more she chooses the Sincere shake and then, to my astonishment, continues our conversation from eight months ago. "So nice to see you again," Hillary smiles. "I've considered our last conversation, at the White House, on poetry, and—"

She remembers we discussed Maya Angelou and e. e. cummings? There's gotta be a wire in her ear, with Secret Service on the other end reading cue cards. I tilt to the left, lean forward, look at her ear. Hillary notices, her raised eyebrows seeming to ask, "Is there bird poop in my hair?"

"Great earrings!" I offer.

· · ·

Smack-dab in the middle of the handshake spectrum is the Cordial Business shake. Two crisp pumps leave shaker and shakee content to either get down to business or depart. I never shook Donald Trump's hand, but I'll bet he's a Cordial. Although I read in a *Playboy* interview that he hates shaking. I think he said it was "a disgusting ritual, spreading all those germs around." *Spreading all those unspoken messages around* is how I see it. It's said that the handshake originated in medieval times, when men would extend their hands to show they had no weapons, a gesture of openness and vulnerability. Perhaps The Donald has a stiletto up his sleeve?

. . .

I thought I'd sampled the complete range of shakes until encountering the I'm Hanging in There for the Long Haul shake. This one features a few dozen up-down pumps, a lengthy—like 15 minutes or more—handholding session coupled with extended, earnest conversation. Leaning against the creamy wall of the White House ballroom, I'm watching President Bill Clinton work the crowd.

"Have you noticed he doesn't let go of the pretty young women?" a man approaches me, grinning beneath bushy gray brows.

"Oh, um, no, I hadn't," I lie.

"I've been to many White House gatherings, and I always observe this ritual. Amusing, no?" He introduces himself as a Nobel laureate.

"Give it a try," he gestures forward. "I'll stay here and do field research," he chuckles, nudges me to motion.

Crossing the room, I reach Bill moments after his last Long Haul shake ends. We smile, we grasp, and we're off. Here I am, not sure whether we're at midshake. It's been 10 minutes and my arm is starting to ache. Women glare at me, like I'm hogging the president. I'm not. I wanted a simple shake 'n' howdy and now I'm stuck. Do I have to wait until the president lets go? What would Miss Manners do?

I smile, chat, and tug, ever so gently, to release. Bill begins up-down pumping. Are we starting from scratch? And now, to complicate matters, I have to pee. Badly. I need an action item, an excuse to say, "I'll get back to you on that, Mr. President. Tally ho!" Okay, "tally ho" isn't appropriate, but my arm is throbbing and turning cold. It's my right arm, my really important arm, my key-to-earning-my-livelihood arm. I press my legs together, as my bladder's screaming has grown insistent. The four Secret Service agents behind the president stare at me, stony faced. They have seen it all before. *Release me. Please.* I mentally beseech the CEO of America.

He doesn't seem to notice, or if he does, he still wants to hold hands so I am out of luck. But he's the president, and, well is this *appropriate*? This holding me hostage with his presidential power? He's taller than me, and he holds my hand higher than is natural. It's starting to look a bit bluish. It's tingling from lack of blood, turning colder. I straighten up, beg into Bill's sparkly eyes. "Mr. President, we need to encourage entrepreneurship in America."

"How would y' do that, Christine?"

"Oh . . . lots of ways."

"Such ayas?"

"A . . . uh, proposal. Yes, I'll write a proposal for you, enumerate my ideas . . . "

"Ahlright, Ah'll look forward to thayat."

"Great meeting you, Mr. President. I'll get to work right away." I yank free my numb, leaden hand, smiling and bowing a little. I spin on my heel, eager to exit, but he dives in for an encore.

"Ahm lookin' forward to your proposal." He nods.

Okay, now I really, *really* have to go. Time to be a little rude.

What would Michael Milken do? "Oh! There's Stephen Hawking! I've been searching for him all night," I twist, pull free, beat a hasty retreat to the restroom.

Hot water gushes from the golden tap, soothes my aching arm. I glance in the mirror. These handshakes have made me feel like an annoying flea, a proud eagle, and an obligated hooker. Do mine send similar messages of disgust, sincerity, or lechery? Pondering this, I notice the hand towels. Hmm . . . soft paper with the presidential seal embossed in gold . . . fabulous souvenir potential. I stash three in my purse, reapply my smile, sashay back to the party.

"Christine, Joe Bernsby, great to meet you!" A bull-like man thrusts a fleshy, sweating hand into my freshly washed one. "*Loved* your speech at the Department of Defense."

"Thank you," I say, wincing a little. Glancing over his shoulder, I think, *Isn't there someone more interesting here?*

Later I seek refuge in the Red Room, remorse sweeping over me. A sincere man had expressed appreciation, and I'd dismissed him. Haven't I learned anything? I apologize in my mind to the moist man, and recall the shake I want to master, the one that makes people feel special.

. . .

"Hi," I say crouching before the seated man. He's alone, slumped over the little desk attached to his wheelchair. "Your speech was terrific," I tell him. "You make physics so . . . accessible. Thanks." He smiles and shifts a little, preparing to type a reply into his speech synthesizer. Aware of the effort I say, "You needn't respond."

He looks up at me, into me, with deep dark eyes—no black holes here. His eyes embrace me in a down-duvet hug. And there it is: connection. I can feel his anguish, his giant, potent mind trapped in a tiny, twisted body. I no longer care that I'm not a player, that I lack real jewels and couture gowns, that I'll probably never be all that important. Because my quest for success has been about being seen, about banishing the perpetual feeling of invisibility and inconsequence, about making sure I matter. And right now, I do. I feel seen all the way through.

And I realize that this . . . this is the moment that I'll remember most—not attending a White House party, not shaking hands with the wealthy and well known, not breaking free from Bill Clinton—but this very real, better-than-a-handshake moment: the soul shake, the touchless shake, of Professor Stephen Hawking.

As I walked from the White House to my hotel I reflected on this experience. I wondered, what did my handshakes say? Did they convey sincerity or rote, robotic disinterest? How often was I paying attention when I interacted with people? Was I just going through the motions, not really connecting with the person but interacting with whatever they represented to me—or whatever my snap judgment had determined? I decided to change, then and there, as I walked along Pennsylvania Avenue, wind whipping my overcoat. I decided to take that risk, that leap, to shed my social mask and show myself to others. Maybe they'd show me who they were in exchange.

In the end, you want a Rolodex you can connect with, not one you can "work." I hate it when someone calls me and says woodenly, "So tell me, um, . . . Christine . . .

how is your husband, um . . . Chris . . . doing?" They
don't know me; they just jotted down some reminder
notes in their contacts database. The caller is a stranger
seeking a favor. I want the kind of relationships where I
smile every time I flip through my Rolodex because my
eyes have fallen on a name I cherish.

First, learn to love networking. As you meet people,
relationships will follow. I'll never stop building relationships—it's so fun and fulfilling. I use my LinkedIn
network (www.linkedin.com) of over a million people
so I can check in with business colleagues when I need
to hire talent, connect my friends to people who'll help
them, and find friends of friends who will introduce
me to people I want to know. I use Plaxo (www.plaxo.com)
to keep my contacts' information up to date.

Connecting people is like chemistry class. I put this
and that together and see what happens. Sometimes it
explodes, but usually it works out. Something better is
created. That's why I say *life = the people you meet + what you
create together.* Whether it's friendships, jobs, companies,
products, families, fund-raisers, or pool parties, life is
about bringing people together and seeing what happens.

ESSENTIALS FOR NETWORKING

1. *Equalize yourself with others.* Remember how we all
   have one unit of self-worth? This means we're all
   equal. Just because people are powerful, rich, or fa-

mous doesn't mean they are better than you. Practice equalizing yourself with others; remembering this will enable you to more comfortably interact with others.

2. *Build your networking momentum.* Talk to people . . . all the time, in line at the store, at the salon, on an airplane. Remember my story about standing in line at Starbucks and meeting someone who wanted to start a new company? I've met amazing mentors, started businesses, and made new friends simply by striking up a conversation. Not sure how to start? Offer a compliment. There's always something attractive or admirable to notice about a stranger. Be sincere about it.

3. *Rolodex dip.* This is a fun practice when you want to connect with someone but aren't sure who. Flip through your contact database until you find a name that makes you smile. Then call that person up just to see how he or she is. Your contact will be surprised and delighted.

4. *Daily appreciation.* Appreciate at least one person daily. I often do this via e-mail, so I can be thorough; often, to my delight, the recipients will tell me that they are saving the message when they need a pick-me-up. You can also express appreciation over the phone or in person. Simply tell others how much you

(continues)

appreciate who they are, what they do, whatever about them moves you. They'll be flattered, and you'll feel great.

5. *"Sensei of the day.*? Each day I pick a sensei, a teacher. This is someone who has taught me a lesson or reminded me of something important in life. Your sensei can be a person, a pet, a plant, it doesn't matter. The important thing is to acknowledge that there is much to learn and you are being offered valuable lessons constantly.

6. *Join a networking group.* Service groups (like Rotary and Kiwanis clubs), industry associations, and job function/title groups (such as associations for marketing professionals) are great places to learn the basics of networking, to meet new friends, and to help foster other people's career dreams. Washington, Jefferson, Rockefeller, and Carnegie all were members of mastermind groups. You should be too. As mentioned in Chapter 2, a mastermind group is a team of like-minded people who come together regularly to help support one another's goals. (Check out the resources on RulesForRenegades.com, too.) I am in two writing mastermind groups, where I've learned about self-editing, story structure, pacing, point of view, and lots more. In my business mastermind group, I've explored new business models for online services and Internet marketing, how to hold a teleseminar, and how to market a book.

7. *Find mentors, advisors, and friends to share goals with.* Searching out mentors, building relationships with people in your field, figuring out how to get on the party-invite lists, and asking the publicity people in your company to share information about increasing your exposure are all good ideas. Think about how you present yourself, which is something that anyone at any level can work on. Setting up a monthly lunch with colleagues from other companies in your field, making a plan to meet someone who can teach you things (or swap services—one woman is helping me with a project in exchange for my providing business consulting to her)—all this is superhelpful.

8. *Do the Drive-By Schmooze.* Parties, conventions, and groups of all sorts are great opportunities, but sometimes you'll be tired, not in the mood, or have too many events in one evening. This is when you'll need to use the Drive-By Schmooze.

   a. *Timebox your networking.* Decide that in 30 minutes you'll do a check-in to determine if you need to stay any longer.

   b. *Let your intuition guide you.* Okay, some of you may think this sounds flaky. Just try it though. Stand near the door, in a corner, or out of the way. Stop your thoughts. Internally ask to be guided to

(continues)

the people you need to connect with. Then start walking. You'll be amazed at who you meet.

c. *Make connections.* Approach a person or group of people, introduce yourself, ask each person what he or she does for a living. Be genuinely interested.

d. *Watch for the person you resonate with.* You'll always resonate with someone. When you do, ask the two most important networking questions: How did you get started in your field? What's your ideal customer? We all love to talk about ourselves, and these questions will not only help you form a connection with this person but will also tell you how to help him or her.

e. *Offer help and follow through.* If you can provide help, jot down ideas on the back of the person's business card, commit to follow up, and then do it. If you've had a fruitful conversation and want to take it further, offer to meet for lunch or coffee. Again, follow through!

COOL FREE RESOURCES

Go to www.RulesForRenegades.com and download "Accountability Partner Worksheet," "Mastermind Group Worksheet," and "How to Create an Advisory Board."

Only You Can Lead Your Life

*Exploring the Guru's Spell—
the Guru with the Meditation
Cushions and the One with
the Nerdy Horn Rims*

*Leadership is a privilege to better the
lives of others. It is not an opportunity
to satisfy personal greed.*

MWAI KIBAKI
president of Kenya

I F YOU'RE READING this book, you're either thinking about being a leader or you are one already. Regardless, leadership isn't all about fat compensation packages, corporate perks, and scraping sycophants. Leadership can be messy, can lack glamour, and can get down and dirty at times. Let's dive in.

A leader is someone whom people choose to follow, and although leadership is an ability we are born with, many of us have to cultivate the ability in order to make it effective. Not everyone who is in charge is a leader. Sometimes entrepreneurs are leaders; sometimes they aren't. Managers are not necessarily leaders; they're administrators. Management skills can be learned, and they certainly are useful. And a leader may not be a great manager.

The inherent tension of leadership is the challenge of just doing things your way or soliciting and incorporating the suggestions of your top lieutenants. The price of leadership is high. You have to make the big decisions, take the big risks, put your neck on the chopping block, and guide people who may be difficult or uncooperative. Leaders also struggle with the inherent tension between their innate desire to lead and their fantasy of letting the reins go now and then. Heck, let's admit it—

some days it's nice to just follow. However, the follower pays an equally high price, though it can be hard to see. Followers don't have the benefit of seeing the big picture; they don't see the business with the 360-degree view that leaders strive for. And that's the most fascinating view in business.

Wherever you fit in your organization, think like a chief executive officer, because let's face it: you are the leader of your life. Who are you going to lead in your own life? Yourself. When you're discouraged, you will "lead" that feeling in a more positive direction. When you're feeling insecure, you will "lead" that emotion by listing all the things you're secure about. Yes, leaders need followers. And that includes your ability to rise above and guide your negative emotions and thoughts into a more positive place. This is the only way to truly take 100 percent responsibility for your life.

More overt ways of leading your life come up all the time at work. You're in charge of convincing your boss you deserve that promotion, managing a project you've been assigned, finding the right job, and dealing professionally with difficult situations at work. Most of all, you have to be in charge of finding out who you are and rocking your career and life.

But rocking your career and life requires gaining emotional equity with others. This is how I see it:

Energy = Equity
Equity = Access
Access = Influence

Putting *energy* into your relationships with people helps to build emotional *equity*, a personal bond, which results in people caring about one another and wanting to contribute to one another's welfare. This degree of *equity* then increases *access* to a person's time, information, and contacts. Increased access enables you to boost your level of *influence* on situations and outcomes. *Influence* enables you to get things done. Every person who gets things done successfully understands the connection between *energy, equity, access,* and *influence*.

I can't tell you how often people tell me that they avoid the colleagues they've labeled as difficult. Then they complain that they can't get these people to help them get things done. Of course not! They have no emotional equity with them.

No One Else Can Lead Your Life: Finding Your Inner Jungle Guide

An Oscar-winning actress recently told me she'd always looked to others to tell her who to be, in both her career and in her personal life. Someone would inevitably show up with a "script" of who she should be at that time. It wasn't until she was approaching 60 years of age that she said "Whoa! It's time to figure out who I am, what I want, and what matters to me." Letting someone else define your destiny, your persona, and your pace in life is pricey—and it's a mistake many of us make at one point or another in our lives. We make it because we lack self-esteem and thus have a propensity for building shrines to the powerful people in our lives. Here's my misadventure with letting someone else lead my life.

We Buddhist monks live and work in the world, which is how I wind up with a job at a bank and get hip to assets. When I start to mouth off a little and tell my meditation teacher, Rama, that he needs to reduce the excessive tithing so his students can acquire assets, he decides that the best way to get me to shut up is to send me on a harrowing trip to the L.A. County morgue. It works. I now remember why I wanted to be a monk in the first place: to reduce human suffering. Mentally taping my mouth shut, I crawl back to Rama, trying to insinuate myself once again into his good graces. The idea that I can help reduce human suffering or make a difference in the world without his assistance never crosses my mind. I drop my high-powered job at the bank. I want to become small, to become nonthreatening, to stop standing out. There's only one leader here, and it ain't me.

I return to college and learn to program. But stifling who I am isn't working. I keep trying to stay small, but I really want to be big, I *need* to speak my mind, chart my own course. The way Rama treats everyone is tricky: he picks favorites and plays us off against one another. One week I'm the golden child; he holds me up as a shining example. Everyone fawns over me. The next week I'm the fallen one; I'm "low vibe" and everyone avoids me. And he always wants more money. I again start questioning his finances, why he now fosters discord among the monks, why the ashram is so competitive. The message I receive is clear: you're not following. You've failed. Bad monk! Rama kicks me out of the ashram.

The bad news? I'm poor, with no savings whatsoever. It's time to start building a financial base for my future, now that I no longer have to fork over so much cash to my teacher. The good news? By working four jobs I won't have time to think about my future, now that my surrogate family/father/friends are gone. It's an excellent way to avoid confronting my feelings and fears—which are substantial.

I followed a guru initially because he inspired me, but over time inspiration was downgraded to fear. There I was again, looking *out* instead of looking *within*—not being the author of my own life. I was disappointed with where I was led and disappointed with not being a leader when, truth be told, I was a lousy follower. I want to be clear: leaders aren't better than followers. If following or implementing someone else's vision is what feels right to you, by all means do it. The world needs team players and team managers both. It just helps to figure out whether you're the right person in the wrong position. You'll do more good and feel better inside your skin when you're in the right place in your organization—or out on your own, if it makes more sense to *be* the leader because you can't *follow* one. You might fit different roles in different cultures; perhaps you're a leader at your company and a follower in your book group.

When you join a company, suss out its culture. What are its tribal customs? Its ceremonial costumes? How deep in do you want to go? It's possible to give a new job your all without giving up your mental and emotional independence. Remember, you are the leader of your own life, and no one else can do it for you. It's great to be part of a company whose mission you believe in, but it's perilous to give total allegiance to your boss simply because he or she is in a position of power. Be willing to look the part, to embrace the mission, but don't buy the whole program if you don't believe it. And please be clear about why you're making your choices; every compromise has a cost. I still remember the boss at my contract programming gig for Domino's Pizza. He constantly hectored me to "be more like Doug," his favorite engineer. I tried to be like Doug briefly—maybe he did things better than I did. Maybe I could somehow get smarter, like he was. Then I saw there was a difference between self-improvement and self-compromise (or even self-annihilation). So I stopped trying to be like Doug and worked on being the best Christine I could.

Whether you want to lead others or not, you can use leadership skills to get where you want to go in life and business—whether you are at the top or the bottom of an organization. Look to work with people who show leadership qualities, spend time with them, model yourself after them, ask them to mentor you. Learn from the leaders around you. Following itself isn't bad—it's the following blindly that'll get you in trouble every time. Sometimes you'll have to pay your dues, but don't get so sucked into the culture that you go native when your intention was to be an anthropologist.

Geeks Gone Wild

I had latent leadership qualities, and while I was developing them, I followed. You can't lead a company until you have an idea for one, or until you've earned your chops by working your way up within a corporation. I learned a lot about leadership at Microsoft. The culture was that of constantly looking for new opportunities. Microsoft made its employees part of its vision of the future, which egged everyone on and kept us working long hours and giving our all. Having a charismatic leader who wasn't afraid to do things differently and challenged his employees helped a lot too. Of course, now and then we were pushed a little too hard.

The first thing I noticed at Microsoft was that it appeared to be every bit as culty as Rama's ashram: everyone lived together, worked together, wanted to get in the leader's good graces, gave over their will and dreams to those of the leader. We all dressed alike, thought alike, had similar hobbies, enjoyed similar entertainment, supported the group goal. We'd probably have slept together more if we weren't so damned tired from working all the time. I felt like a Stepford Wife with a motherboard instead of an apron. My life was all about "the cause," and at Microsoft that meant a PC running Microsoft software on every desktop and in every home.

The best part about working at Microsoft was all the smart people I met. They looked like followers on the outside, but many of them had gigs on the side. When they weren't at the office they were doing contract jobs for other companies or were building their own start-ups. They were hedging their bets. I wanted to do this too, to study leadership at Microsoft until I could have my own company one day. I kept my eyes and options open, so when a headhunter called about a path out of software testing and into programming at Lotus, I jumped. I learned two important things at Microsoft. One, that sometimes you'll have to leave your current job (or plan to) in order to be taken seriously for a promotion. That's how I finally transitioned from testing to coding. And two, that I wasn't cut out for business cults. I was first and foremost an entrepreneur—someone who needs to do her own thing, who's lousy at office politics and butt kissing, who'd rather speak her mind than play the diplomat. I wasn't a leader yet, but I was beginning to see what one does.

Dos and Don'ts of Leadership

When you're with a real leader and you know he or she is being straight with you, you'll follow that person through jungles rife with savage beasts. So grab your machete. We're going into the thicket.

LEADERS BUILD A ROCKIN' TEAM

If you're an entrepreneur, your team will need to cover all areas of business: sales, marketing, operations/finance, leadership (CEO), product development, and so on. If you're an intrapreneur, you'll likely know the positions you need. Still, you'll want to do the following things.

1. *Hire the Fantastic Four.* Your Fantastic Four will be visionaries, leaders, implementers, and infrastructure builders/supporters.

   - *Visionaries* must be highly visible and articulate; these people will "see" the future of the products or services of your company as well as new markets you should enter. They'll wow prospective clients, financiers, and upper management.

   - *Leaders* will likely be in executive management; they have the gift to make their mission everyone else's. A great leader can inspire and motivate people to do anything.

   - *Implementers* make things happen. They build the products or services, they market them, and they sell them.

   - *Infrastructure builders/supporters* will create the foundation, processes, and procedures of the company to keep it running smoothly and enable it to grow.

2. *Rock the culture.* The best way to build, support, and retain a great team is to encourage a rockin' culture that everyone wants to be part of. Your company or team should have values that everyone agrees to uphold. These should be posted visibly on the wall,

placed to remind people. Here are ours at Mighty Ventures:

Take 100 Percent Responsibility for Your Work and Life

Provide Five-Star Client Service

Live I-R-S: Initiative, Responsibility, Speed

Make a Difference at Work and in the World

Everyone throughout the organization must be empowered to support one another in upholding the company values. Culture doesn't last long if it is merely sloganeering. Sure, you can call your employees "associates," but if they're treated poorly, don't be surprised if they scoff at their inflated titles and dis the corporate culture.

3. *Choose your team wisely.* Look for these attributes:

- *Smarts.* Hire the smartest people you can find, preferably smarter than you. They'll find their way out of the majority of messes they'll get into. It takes guts to do this . . . and you have them!

- *GSD.* Remember that a GSD (Gets Stuff Done) can be far more useful than an MBA. Look to their *accomplishments*, not their advanced degrees.

- *Emotional EQUITY.* We're talking the heavy-duty man/woman-on-a-mission stuff. When the grenades are flying, the committed person doesn't bail. He or she hunkers down and deals with the problem. There is *nothing* more valuable than this commitment, this emotional equity. No amount of stock options or cash compensation even comes close.

- *Plays well with others.* I became an entrepreneur because I *didn't* play well with others. But I learned. And it's been one of the greatest lessons I've ever embraced. We need one another. We all have value. Never forget this.

4. *Build an extended team.* As an intrapreneur, you'll need advisors or mentors in your extended team. These folks will likely not receive any sort of financial compensation, which is further reason for you to build solid emotional equity with them. For more on recruiting mentors and advisors, see the Resources section at the end of this chapter. As an entrepreneur, you'll need investors, board directors, and advisors. Investors will come from creating your capital acquisition strategy (see Chapter 8). Your board of directors should have five to seven people; ideally two investors, the CEO, one other company executive, and people you trust for the rest. Your advisory board should have ten people, max, and include a couple of industry heavyweights, a model customer, and several savvy businesspeople with great connections in the operational areas most crucial to your success. Needless to say, everyone should get stock options (with the exception of the

investors). The amount will range from 0.25 to 3 percent of the total outstanding stock, based on the stage of the company and the amount of work the advisor will do. Filling in an advisory board will take time. Most start-ups don't fill all board seats within the first year of operations. Be picky!

LEADERS ARE ALWAYS COURSE CORRECTING

What does a leader look like to you? Competent, reliable, professional, has a positive attitude, and respect for others? These are the qualities that get you into the game; they're the price of admission. So what'll you do once you get in the door? If there's one thing I've learned about leadership, it's that leaders are always course correcting. If people aren't following them and their directives, they gently guide them back on track. To get people to follow you, you'll need to tell them where to go and then course-correct when they start to stray. You'll also need to course-correct your entire company and, most important, *yourself*. You'll make mistakes, your team will, your customers will, your board will. And you'll fix those mistakes by honestly taking stock and changing the way you do things.

One CEO, Jason, talked his board into taking the company public before it was ready. The second quarter after the initial public offering, the company missed their earnings target. Wall Street was relentless—the stock was hammered —from $26 per share down to $4. What did Jason do? Did he get out on the road, visit customers, sell more product, fly around to the regional sales offices? Nope. He locked himself in his office and wrote ad copy. Would writing a killer ad save his company? I don't think so. Jason became invisible, and everyone knew he was hiding. No course correcting here—not by the CEO, not by the board. Two vice presidents attempted course correction and Jason promptly dismissed them. The situation went from bad to worse. Ultimately, six months too late, Jason was replaced. The company never recovered, and it was sold at a massive discount to a competitor.

A true leader would admit his mistake, rally the troops, reassure the customers, stare down that stock price, and turn it around. He would do this by handling customer and shareholder objections, pumping up the salespeople to keep them focused on closing deals, and buoy the staff to keep them motivated even though their stock was underwater.

A vice president of engineering had an intellectual property fiasco. Two key engineers had quit the company and decided to create a competitive product. The engineers had of course signed employment contracts stating that whatever they developed was the company's property, yet they conveniently chose to forget this. Years later these two engineers—who had raised millions of dollars in financing—had the nerve to lob lawsuits at the company they'd left, claiming patent infringement. The VP was initially freaked out—how could his former staff claim the product he'd paid for was theirs? They were better funded than his company was, and the thought of spending years and all his reserve cash mired in lawsuits left him frozen with fear.

He was worn out and considered throwing in the towel, angry as he was. Once he calmed down and took stock of the situation, he realized it was key to course-correct. He rallied the troops and got them engaged in finding the solution. He led his team through the crisis and quickly uncovered a series of smoking gun memos (in addition to the employment contracts) that supported his company's ownership of the product and patents. His CEO hired a killer intellectual property litigator and lobbed a countersuit their way.

That was the easy part. Now he had to help the vice president of sales with the customers and sales prospects, who feared having their now-entrenched products ripped out of their companies. The CEO refused to let the lawsuits destroy his business, found some new sources of financing, and brought on additional advisors. The team was reinvigorated and ready to rock. Talk about course correction! The VP of Engineering started it, the VP of Sales and CEO furthered it! And only recently were the lawsuits settled in favor of the founding company, resulting in a hefty payment. The unethical engineers were court ordered to cease selling their stolen product. It was a thrill to help the company through this crisis.

Leaders trust their instincts. They know they'll make the best decisions they can at a given time, and they'll course-correct if things don't turn out as planned. Encouraging a culture of course correction leads to the

most effective way to deal with disasters and encourage
risk taking and ownership. In this culture, people know
that no one's head is going to roll if a mistake is made
or a crisis occurs; you're simply going to hunker down
and deal with it. Everyone is going to be accountable for
their actions in a culture that isn't based on blame. Accountability is the first step in ownership. The second
is having control and responsibility for projects. If it's
yours, and you truly own the outcome, you'll knock
yourself out to make it work. This is the only culture
where you can truly develop people—as executives and
as human beings—and it's the best way to foster entrepreneurship in an organization.

LEADERS FOSTER COLLABORATION

Leaders help staff get work done by providing financial
resources, strategic vision and tactical guidance, a solid
working environment, emotional support and coach-
ing, and acknowledgment and credit when and where
due. They know they can't do it alone. They know that
staff members are responsible for at least 75 percent of
all their company's achievements. Sure, successful leaders are glorified in the press and receive meaty compensation packages, but they know who helped them get
there. Leaders need to manage on three levels: up to
their boss (the CEO or the board of directors), down
to their direct reports, and across to their customers
and colleagues in their company, in the industry, in the
media.

Collaboration is key. Some people cling to outdated beliefs such as "the boss is evil," "we're superior to our staff," "the customer needs us more than we need them." This us-versus-them thinking is outdated and unproductive. To rock your business you need to achieve escape velocity, the energy required to bypass entrenched competitors and entrenched ideas. And you can't escape the pull of gravity without others. Look at Starbucks rocketing past Peet's Coffee, Google leaving Yahoo! in the dust, JetBlue scorching the established airlines. That kind of performance takes raw, unbridled energy. You need to get as many people propelling you upward as possible. As Mario Andretti says, "If things seem under control, you are just not going fast enough."

Leaders foster collaboration both externally and internally, and especially with clients and prospects even when it's unpleasant at times. At one of my past companies our two top sales guys had a huge deal in the works. This was a deal of "make-or-break-the-company" proportions. After months of technology assessments and meetings, we met with the key decision maker over dinner to ink the deal.

We were seated at a round table with Fred, the decision maker, on my right. Shortly into the meal, before the appetizers arrived, I felt a hand slide onto my thigh. Looking down I realized it was Fred's. Ick. Sure, I was mortified, but this wasn't the time to cause a scene. Carefully, so as not to attract attention, I lifted Fred's hand off my thigh and dropped it in his lap. A few minutes later it was back on my leg. Puh-lease. What was this guy trying to do? Psych me out? Get me to jump or freak out or blow the deal? Have his way with me? Who cares? We were pursuing a deal, and I had to stay the course. I wasn't about to let my sales guys down. I was glad I had worn a pantsuit, though.

Fred's wandering hand continued throughout the meal, and I continued to remove it. Afterward, as we walked out to the street ahead of the others, he turned to me and said, "There's a terrific strip club nearby. Come with me, and we'll seal the deal."

Guess I passed the first test. Why do a second one? I looked him in the eye, and said, "Gosh, Fred. I've got a lot to do tonight. How about I *don't* go to the strip club and we *do* the deal anyway? I think our guys can handle it from here." He winked, we shook hands, and everything worked out.

Fred turned out to be a decent guy. When his company had a tough time deploying our software in their antiquated environment, we flew our technicians to their site to upgrade their entire system. When we needed preferential payment terms, Fred came through. Needless to say, our sales guys were horrified when I told them about his wandering hand at the dinner, but they appreciated my dealing with Fred's inappropriate behavior and not blowing the deal. Had I done so, the collaborative and mutually beneficial relationship we later built would never have come to be. The moral of the story is, if a deal has terrific potential for collaboration, don't blow it. Navigate any initially weird or tricky trials and keep your eye on the ultimate benefit. Yes, I was grossed out by Fred's bizarre behavior. But it wasn't worth destroying a deal over.

What I sensed in Fred, for all his groping, was that he was going to work with us. I knew that I wasn't going to have to sit next to him every day. But if I'd sensed that he was going to be difficult, or evasive, or confrontational, I would have walked. If the relationship is doomed from the start, don't do the deal. Noncollaborative deals set the tone for your business and staff, and it's a lower standard than you deserve. Disagreement, conflict, or stress all show a person's or business's true colors—anyone who starts out being arbitrary will only get worse when times are bad. Mature, professional businesspeople know that they need one another, and thus they are happy to find a way to make things work.

Another huge benefit of a collaborative environment is that the leader is approachable. She wants to hear the ideas and concerns of her team. She wants her opinions to be challenged and to be shown better ways to do things. A collaborative environment builds emotional equity and results in people giving their best because they care deeply, they know their contribution matters, and they know they'll be acknowledged for it.

LEADERS "HAVE A PAIR"

. . . and they're made of brass. A leader proves this by regularly taking risks, making decisions even if he can't acquire all the necessary information, and fixing mistakes both by himself and his team. Leaders take calculated risks and are always looking to expand their business, never resting on past success.

Building the team is a crucial part of leadership. We'll delve into delegation in Chapter 9, but here's my short list of people-related practices of a great leader:

- She hires people who are smarter than she is or have expertise beyond her own. She realizes she won't have all the answers and that's okay. And she doesn't just hire a few smarties: a good leader *surrounds* herself with people who are smarter than she is. She's not threatened by brains.

- He loves competition. He knows that today's competitor could be tomorrow's business partner, so you won't find him dissing the competition. He'll study it and capitalize on its weaknesses.

- She carries a big umbrella. When problems come raining down, a leader whips out that umbrella and keeps charging ahead. And the umbrella is big enough to keep her staff clean and dry, too. This is especially relevant when you're an intrapreneur.

- He *knows* his people—where they excel, where they struggle, what their next two promotions should be. A great leader helps his people get ahead by putting them in roles where they will grow and

stretch, not sink or simply swim. He coaches
them in new situations, pays attention to see if
they're ok, and course-corrects if they're not.

- She rewards and affirms her staff because she
knows that research repeatedly shows that
acknowledgment and appreciation are the keys to
a happy, motivated, loyal team member. Her
acknowledgment is sincere. She knows businesses
aren't built alone. We need one another to
achieve great things.

- He knows that challenges will stretch him and
help him grow—like dealing with difficult people
and getting them to do what you want, as the
following situation illustrates.

"This company is a train wreck. The CEO is clueless; he's
missed his target for the last three quarters. The business
model is weak, the expenses are entirely too high. I'm mad as
hell." Mack's face looks like raw fatty hamburger, fleshy, pink
and pinched. He's a co-investor in this company with me, and
we're trying to stop the downward spiral. Or, I am, at least.

"I'm not happy about this either, Mack. All of the board
members share your concerns. We have a plan. We're recruiting a new CEO, and I've found a solid candidate. We need to
cut seven staff members to reduce expenses."

"The CEO is one helluva stupid jerk. How can he have had
eight years in sales and fail to meet his quarterly forecast again

and again? The expenses are excessive. This company is a ship just waiting to sink." Now his pink face is turning deep red, like steak tartare.

"Yes, we have messes to clean up. And a plan to do so." *I will keep my cool. I will.*

"And you, your firm invested in this crappy company first and touted it to the rest of us. I'll make sure your name is blacklisted throughout the venture capital community." His cheeks are now the gruesome purple-maroon of an undercooked steak.

"That's an interesting point of view. Your firm did your own due diligence. I didn't even *meet* you until the deal papers were drawn up." *Whoa! Be cool. No need to defend. Breathe. Don't let him get to you—you've seen his bad behavior before: his screaming in board meetings, his trying to crush the confidence of others, his blaming everyone for his lack of action. Breathe. He's just a bully.*

"Well, you told the venture capital community it was a good deal, and our team heard that, and they were influenced, and that was wrong, and..."

"Mack, we've both done investments that looked good, and later found ourselves in deep doo-doo. Then you have a choice: dig in and try to find the pony, or leave the barn. Sounds like you want the latter."

"I want this mess fixed, that's what I want. This airplane is headed for a crash landing."

"Do you really, Mack? All you do is rant about it. So, let's just shut the company down. We can take a couple of million dollars off the table. After paying the creditors, we'll net about 30 cents on the dollar. But it looks like you've given up, and our other board member is AWOL, so we're out of luck." I push my chair back, as if I intend to leave. It's time for the "takeaway close," to call his bluff, to see if he'll finally stop complaining and agree to some action.

"Damn . . ." His countenance returns to steak tartare.

"There is one other alternative, Mack. We merge this company with one that has a stronger business model and recurring revenue. We consolidate the staff, reduce expenses, and maybe even get a million bucks from new investors." *Let's do something, for Chrissakes.*

"Sounds like you have a company in mind. Bet you want to unload another loser on us."

"I know the company, but I don't have any financial interest in it. They have solid revenue and a large customer base, and we can sell our technology into their same accounts. Their sales close in three months, whereas ours take nine. Plus they're out of cash." *I so deserve a massage after this meeting. Totally.*

"Okay, listen up. Here's what we're going to do. We bring in a new CEO and merge with a company with solid sales. I become chairman of the merged company. Over time, we sell our more complex technology into the merger candidate's existing accounts. We consolidate staff and cut expenses. We get a few million bucks of new money invested, and we get a second chance to make this pony run."

"What a great idea, Mack. I'm in."

Was Mack a jerk? Yep. Did I want to achieve a specific result? Yep. Did I have to make my ideas his? Yep. First I had to equalize myself with him, by not placing him above or below me. Then I had to collaborate, I had to course-correct and make him think it was his idea. Because that's the only way to get what's best for everyone when you're dealing with a difficult personality like Mack's.

Here are my Three E's for dealing with difficult people:

Equalize: Place yourself on par with the person in your mind. You both were drooling babies; you both will grow old and die; you both are made of the same stuff.

Exchange: Perhaps the person is suffering in some aspect of life. Maybe this is why the individual is so difficult to deal with. Remember a time when you were struggling and "exchange" your suffering for his or hers.

Embrace: On August 15, 2005 I decided to accept people exactly as they are. This is one of the best decisions I have ever made. Now when I am annoyed by peoples' behavior, I know that I cannot possibly change it. Wishing is futile. So I embrace, or accept, them just as they are. From that vantage point I can choose to interact with them in the future or not. And I won't waste any energy on judging them or wanting them to change.

LEADERS WORK WITH PEOPLE, FOR BETTER OR WORSE

A company is made up of people, and people have that awkward humanity that can interfere with their work. Sometimes you'll have to have the guts to help your team through a tough patch. Many years ago I received a call from one of my top salespeople, Jane. She'd been in the process of a messy divorce and the settlement was now complete—and highly unfavorable. Her kids had been manipulated into testifying against her, and the financial side wasn't much better. Jane felt she'd lost everything: the love of her children, many of her possessions, and her sense of where she fit in life. This was too much for her. She called me and said the only bright spot in life was her job and that wasn't enough—the pain was excruciating. She had a gun. She was trying to find reasons not to blow her brains out.

I listed several reasons, doing the best selling I could, but she wasn't convinced. I resorted to the only option I could think of: I'd fly from our office in Chicago out to her home on the West Coast, we'd talk it through, and then she could make her decision. I wanted one last shot at making my case for her life. She agreed, and I flew a few thousand miles that day. I drove straight from the airport to the park where we'd agreed to meet, rehearsing the reasons to live that I'd written on the plane.

We talked for a few hours. Did I convince her to keep living? I don't know. I simply said what I believed was true: that she had fantastic gifts, that she'd get through this. I told her stories about my life when I saw no end to the horror but had no choice but to keep hanging on because for a Buddhist, suicide solves nothing. I told her about all the people I knew who admired her and enjoyed interacting with her. She chose to live, to take some time off, and to find meaning in her life again.

I learned a cool lesson about personal and team interaction at Second City in Los Angeles recently. Fulfilling a dream, I enrolled in Second City's Comedy Writing Immersion Course. For a week I dove into writing and sharing my beginner's attempts at comedy sketches à la *Saturday Night Live*. When critiquing one another's work. we had to preface all our comments with "what if." What if the middle school teacher was unfazed by the executioner presenting at career day? What if the only voice of reason was a nine-year-old child? "What if" removes ego and emotion when providing feedback. I've used this technique both in business and family interactions, and it is extremely effective: with it people become receptive to your ideas, instead of potentially being threatened by them.

Personal interactions can be hard, possibly painful, but at the end of the day leaders remember it's all about people. Without one another there's no business, no bonuses, no happy clients, no cool accomplishments.

LEADERS SAY IT AND DO IT

Leaders are charismatic. They motivate their teams by sharing big-picture plans, helping their staff understand how the company works, what it cares about, and why. But have you ever been in one of those rah-rah staff meetings and something's out of sync? Like you're watching one of those dubbed *Godzilla* movies and the actor's lips have stopped moving but the dialogue continues?

Sometimes you'll follow a charismatic leader and everything will be okay for a while. Then the dreaded day comes when you have to face it: his words rarely match his results. He isn't keeping his commitments, he isn't cut out for this role, and the excuse meter is squarely in the red. At one company, the CEO had adopted a Vision of the Week. On Friday afternoons he'd bring in beer and pizza and tell everyone about the company's fabulous future. Wild enthusiasm ensued. Then he did the beer-pizza-and-success routine the next Friday. Everybody felt great again. Then key sales failed to come through. But he partied the next Friday anyway, because he'd had an epiphany and here was the "even better" path the company was headed down. Then that path was a dead end, but still, there he was on Friday with the great-future refrain. Then some workers were laid off. But on Friday . . . *again*. Finally the staff got sick of all the talk with no results. They declared mutiny and bailed on him.

This is another reason that you hire people smarter than you. The role of CEO is a lonely job. You want your inner circle to call you on your mistakes, to generate exceptional ideas, to provide a sanity check if things get insane. Always, always, have a trusted sounding board. Then have the guts to listen to it. Leaders have the humility to realize they don't have all the answers.

LEADERSHIP TIPS, *NOT* LEADERSHIP HEAD TRIPS

1. Results can coexist with compassionate leadership, and compassionate leadership doesn't mean you're a pushover.

2. Remember that true leaders are always elevating the status of others. Think of all the ways you can raise the status of your team. Then do it.

3. You can have it all; you'll just need to adjust your expectations. And don't expect to have it all at the same time.

4. Make the best decisions you can and course-correct constantly.

5. Foster collaboration: see *everyone* as a potential business partner. People who are problematic one day may be your best allies the next—don't give up on them too quickly.

6. Get mentors and sounding boards and listen to what they say. Study and model successful leaders.

7. Hire people who are smarter than you, capitalize on the competition's weaknesses, and carry a big umbrella to protect your team.

8. You're working with people. They will have personal problems that may affect their performance. Do what you can to help them through these.

9. Don't sacrifice yourself to the cause: ensure that you are paid well, get the respect you deserve, and have a personal life.

10. Say it and *do* it. If you can't, cop to it and explain the situation.

11. Leaders will be criticized. Deal with it. Do what's right, and the slash of criticism won't cut you. Look in the mirror and like the person you see.

COOL FREE RESOURCES

Go to www.RulesForRenegades.com and download "Effective Board Reporting," "Goal Setting Worksheet," "Building Your Dream Team Worksheet," "Assessing Your Leadership Potential," and "How to Create An Advisory Board."

Work Your Money Mojo

Why CEO Really Means Cash Extraction Officer

Money is better than poverty, if only for financial reasons.

WOODY ALLEN

I'LL BE THE FIRST to admit that the ins and outs of financing are enough to make my eyes glaze over. But you've got to be financially literate, my renegade friend, so this chapter is necessary. It's not as lively as the others, but it is jam-packed full of practical, bottom-line info you'll need to finance your company or internal project.

"Cash is king," as they say. Your company's money is its lifeblood. Sure, you can get by for a little while by bootstrapping your company and running on a shoestring budget. But to achieve rapid and sustained growth, sooner or later you'll probably have to attract financiers. Whether you're the CEO of a start-up, raising money to fund your dream, or an intrapreneur "CEO" lobbying for internal funding, CEO means *cash extraction officer.* This chapter gives you the tips and tactics you'll need to get what you want.

Darts? Or Magic 8-Ball? Too many people seem to use one (or both!) of these time-honored techniques when seeking funding. *This is insane.* If you don't develop a solid capital acquisition strategy, you're likely to get the wrong money at the wrong time from the wrong financiers on the wrong terms. Let's suppose you've got a terrific business plan thanks to the tips in Chapter 3 and you've honed your 20-minute financing pitch. You've built a great team with some of the advice in Chapters 6 and 7. Now all you need is cash. That's what I craved after starting Kuvera, back in Chapter 1.

Inhale. Exhale. Inhale. It's two weeks since I launched Kuvera and landed 35 employees overnight. The first payroll is about to hit, and my bank balance is $2,000. Luckily, it's a partial pay period. Hey, I only need $44,000 more to pull this off. This wouldn't be an issue if Microsoft had paid my first invoice, which I'd hand-delivered to Dick a week ago. Time to start calling him by his proper name. Time to start kissing up. Time to place a collections call.

"Hi, Richard, how're you? It's Christine." I commence my positive thinking mantra: *I like this man. He is nice. He will help me.* Repeat.

Silence. Then, "Yeah, what do you want?"

"I just noticed that we haven't received payment for our previous invoice. When shall we expect it?" *Think positive. "Soon, Christine," is what he'll say. "I was just authorizing the payment, Christine."*

"Listen, Christine, this is Microsoft. We pay when we want to. You have a problem with that, you work with someone else." Click.

Okay, so maybe he's not ready to receive my positive mental messages. Maybe he's thinking something more along the lines of "Break her before she gets started. Break her. Break her. Break her."

Time for my Plan B: cash advances on my credit cards. I max out Visa. I need $22,000 more. Then I max out Mastercard. I still need $8,000 more. Next, I max out Discover Card. Bingo! I make payroll, with $1.05 to spare. No problem: I have a whole two weeks to fund the next payroll.

I have to figure out how to raise $80,000 more within two weeks, since no way is Dick—I mean Richard—going to send me a check. A week later I'm a few pounds lighter, since I have no money for food. While I'm pushing panic away, my inner critic—the vile bitch upstairs—joins the party, trying to psych me out. I generate tons of ideas to act on, figuring at least one will work. Will the head of HR pry Richard's talons off my invoices? Yes. She gets them routed to accounts payable. There they start to gather dust. Ultimately, I have to elevate the issue to Bill Gates. He says I must have ticked Richard off (ya think?), but he'll try to grease the skids for me. And suddenly, my past-due invoices are all paid up—one *day* before the $80,000 payroll is due. Sheesh, that was close.

––––––––––––

In addition to maxing out my credit cards, I funded my own companies lots of ways: I factored invoices (several times—don't worry, I'll explain it), used a bank credit line (constantly), and took venture capital (once). There are four basic avenues entrepreneurs explore for financing: (1) sales of the product or service, (2) a loan from an individual or an institution, (3) a grant from the government or an institution, and (4) selling equity in the company. You should read about the avenue that's most likely for you first, and then go back and review the others. Your funding strategy may be a combination of a lot of different sources, and that's okay. It's good to diversify: a blend of equity and debt is a great idea. I'll start with financing your dream without going to someone else for money.

If you're an intrapreneur, it is likely that you'll have to lobby for funds by cost justifying your project. You can go to www. RulesForRenegades.com and read all the return-on-investment (ROI) resources, because there's a lot to learn about internal competition for projects. Sure, you'll be competing with other expenses, but there's more to it than that—the "soft" issues of inertia, internal politics, and resistance to change can tighten a company's financial fist faster than you can say "gimme."

The rest of this chapter focuses on raising money from outside of a company. However, many of the principles are the same, whether you're inside or outside. That is, you need to prove that you have a viable product; you need to set measurable goals that will help you track your progress and report it to management, and you need to internalize the core of entrepreneurship: innovative risk taking. Since dollars for internal projects have become increasingly tight, I recommend you at least read through the 3C's below for "funding" ideas.

> ## 3 Cs of Funding from Within: Customers, Consulting, Cost Control
>
> *Upside: you control your destiny and equity*
> *Downside: you control your destiny and equity*

CUSTOMERS

One of the most traditional ways to fund your company is to have your customers fund your growth. Wow! What a concept. In the days of the high-tech Internet boom, entrepreneurs all but forgot what spurred a lot of the biggest businesses: selling products to customers and funneling the revenue back into the company's operations and development. This is a great way to maintain control of your company and generate positive cash flow.

One of the start-up companies I've worked with had a customer who needed its sales executives to be more effective at managing their third-party resellers. The start-up company had a sales-force compensation product that, with a few enhancements, would solve the customer's problem beautifully. The trouble was, the start-up didn't have the funding to take on this project. The solution? Negotiate with the customer, who agreed to fund the product development. We knew that in time the start-up could sell this enhanced product to other companies, so it was worth what initially appeared to be a distraction. The customer paid $200,000 for the product enhancements and agreed to license it on an annual basis. The start-up agreed to give the customer an exclusivity period, meaning that it wouldn't sell the product to a short list of direct competitors for 90 days.

Customer-funded product development deals have come in handy many times. The biggest one I've seen was $800,000 from a chip manufacturer to fund the development of key technology that it licensed from one of our start-ups. You usually need a couple of customers first so that the funding customer has confidence in your ability to deliver. You also need sophisticated board members or advisors to help you negotiate the deal if you haven't done one before. If you must offer an exclusivity period, start with three months. If you have to increase that to six months to get the deal done, make sure it makes business sense—get a guaranteed order size (and make it BIG). And, of course, have your attorney involved in the entire process so he or she can make sure product ownership is abundantly clear. You own it, and the customer licenses it for a period of time. You'll also want to make sure you're filing patents for any key technology you develop.

CONSULTING

If you can offer consulting services to fund the cost of operations and product development, do it. Your knowledge can be a valuable commodity. In the first example above, the start-up provided consulting on how to compensate both internal and external sales forces, how to track sales quotas, and how to administer payments.

Many start-ups have self-funded this way. Later, when the company was ready to release its first product, it was already in a great financial position with existing sales; solid, happy customers; and a nice cash cushion. It had maintained full ownership and control of the company because it had not needed outside investors. Now it could choose to take on equity or debt financing, and the company would have a higher value.

Cost Control

Whenever you can cut costs without reducing your ability to develop and sell products or services, do it. Potential financiers will want to know your "burn rate"—the rate at which your company is consuming cash on a monthly basis. Knowing this helps financiers evaluate the current and projected amount of cash your company will require for general operations. If, for instance, your company has significant infrastructure expenses or complicated manufacturing, your financing needs will be larger and your deal will be scrutinized more closely. In this case, you'll have to justify all significant expenses and offer ideas for reducing them.

When I say "all significant expenses," I mean it. Don't neglect the obvious. Full-time employees are expensive. Several roles can be filled by either part-timers or hourly contractors. For sales and marketing needs, several companies I know have hired unemployed actors on an hourly basis. Actors are great at reading scripts and infusing their voice with enthusiasm, and if managed properly, they can generate and qualify sales leads over the phone. Take the ones with the strongest selling skills, the ones who are comfortable asking for sales orders, and have them do telephone- or Web-based sales. Give them a quota. In my previous companies, we even used contract salespeople and paid them commission only—20 to 25 percent on their sales. Contractors may not be as committed as employees, but you can offer incentives to increase their loyalty and commitment. Pay them bonuses based on results, refer other clients to them, and keep your company at the top of your contractors' minds by knowing what your contractors care about and helping them achieve their goals. If you are a key source of business for them, they'll have a lot at stake in maintaining the relationship.

Customer support is another area where you can hire contractors or outsource the function entirely. Have experienced project leaders evaluate and manage lower-rate contractors. As long as you have someone whom you can trust running a given department (see "Leaders Build a Rockin' Team" in Chapter 7), encourage the hiring of contractors—and convey a sense of accountability for cost-cutting measures across the company.

Check out www.elance.com, www.craigslist.org, and www.teamdoubleclick.com to find contractors with all varieties of skill sets. Ask around, too. Through friends we found a guy based in India for graphic design, marketing materials, and Web site design work. He does terrific work at a reasonable price.

Stalking the Wild Funder: Your Capital Acquisition Strategy

When taking outside funding—or when determining if you even want to—you'll first need to develop a capital acquisition strategy. To do so, ask yourself the following questions.

STEP ONE:
HOW MUCH DO YOU NEED?

Rule One: Take more than you think you need.
Rule Two: Do so only if it's cheap.

Cash is cheap, equity is not. Once you sell a percentage of your company, recovering it is very difficult and very expensive. This is why multiple smaller financing rounds are a great idea, especially in the start-up phase when your company's value is low. Figure out how much money you need to raise to achieve some specific time-measured milestones such as launching your product, expanding your sales force, and implementing new manufacturing methods. Add that number to your overall operational costs. Now add a cushion of six to nine months of operational costs to that. This is roughly how much you need to raise. The point is to have enough money to both keep the company running and achieve specific milestones so you can demonstrate increased value before you're out fund-raising again.

STEP TWO:
WHEN DO YOU NEED IT?

Rule One: Raise money before you need it.
Rule Two: This will be sooner than you think.

The financing process always takes longer than anticipated. For bank loans, expect two to three months. For Small Business Administration (SBA) loans, expect four to six months. For angel investment or venture capital, expect three to 12 months. I've seen financings occur in less time, but you must be prepared for the long haul.

Start raising money six to nine months before you're either due to run out of cash or expect to need it for expansion. Have a strong banking relationship already established in the event that you need a bridge loan to tide you over during an extended financing process. Respectable jumps in your company's value are expected between financing rounds. In the early stages, at least a two- to threefold increase is expected. You'll need to be able to demonstrate evidence that you've hit some milestones, such as more customers, new products and services (or new versions of already existing ones), and increased market share.

If you schedule your financing rounds when you can show demonstrable success, you'll garner higher valuations and you will be able to keep your investors and staff happy.

Step Three: From Whom Do You Want It?

Rule One: Only take money from someone you like and respect.
Rule Two: Invest the time to find this out.

You'll be with your financiers for two to seven years. You'll go through heaven and hell together. Make sure there will be good company at both venues. In addition, it's preferable to find financiers who understand the industry sector your company serves. Make a list of ten financiers who understand your market or product, invest at the stage your company is currently at, and have portfolio companies that would benefit your product or service. To find financiers, Google for "venture capital," "business loans," "micro loans," or "angel investors" in your geographical area, or go to www.angelcapital education.org and click on Info for Entrepreneurs. Approach the top five on your list. If you've done your homework and you get lucky, you'll stop there. If not, approach the other five.

Never tell prospective venture capitalists about one another. If some decide they don't want to invest, they may call the others and mess up your deal. With banks and angel investors, this advice doesn't apply. If your company is not garnering interest, revisit Chapter 3 to make sure you've located a painful problem and your solution to it is stated in a concise, compelling, and complete way. If it is, then pursue more financiers. If it's not, you may need to retrench and be a quick-change artist, as we discussed in Chapter 1.

Do you want "active" or "passive" money? Active money is from financiers who will work with you closely.

They'll add value by introducing you to sales prospects, influential people such as potential mentors and members of the media, and more. Passive money is just money —no connections, no additional value. If your company is at the seed or early stage, or if the financier has key contacts you need to tap, take active money. If you already have enough active connections and just need cash, take passive funding. Investor relations can be time consuming. Plan for this.

STEP FOUR:
WHAT COMPROMISES WILL YOU ACCEPT?

Rule One: Don't be greedy.
Rule Two: But don't be taken advantage of either.

Since you'll be selling pieces of your company repeatedly, as the pie gets bigger the increased number of pieces get smaller—unless you're financing *Springtime for Hitler* from the movie *The Producers.* This is called *dilution.* If you start out by owning 50 percent of a company, prefinancing, don't be surprised if you own 10 percent or less years later at the exit. In the beginning you will sell off big pieces, often 20 to 40 percent per financing. I personally don't like selling more than 33 percent. I figure if you're going to sell a big piece, sell it for a high price.

Loss of equity is one compromise; loss of control is another. Investors should comprise 20 to 40 percent of the board. Having more is asking for trouble. I've seen way too many cases where the investors ran the company because they controlled the board. This situation rarely works out. I've also seen too many cases where the entrepreneur wanted a far higher valuation than she deserved and either lost valuable time to market or lost the financing altogether by greedily stretching the deal. And lastly, it's worth taking a lower valuation to get a stronger group of investors. Strong, active investors can make all the difference—not only in helping build the company but also in participating in future financing rounds and helping raise cash when the chips are down.

Valuation is emotional. Valuation is based on perception. If your company is presented well, with great passion, a solid executive team, and a good plan to make your vision a reality, the results can be delightful—and surprising. Always be building the value of your company. This will boost your ability to secure preferable financing terms as well as a lucrative exit.

Traditional Sources of Funding

The high-level categories here are lending or equity-based financing. We'll start with the many types of lending.

Bank and SBA Loans

Upside: They are debt only.
Downside: They can be hard to get; paperwork can be excessive.

Banks. Determine which bank in your community understands the type of company you have. For example,

Wells Fargo and Comerica in San Francisco are great banks for biotech and technology companies. In the San José area, Silicon Valley Bank and Cupertino National Bank work extensively with entrepreneurs. Once you have a relationship established with the bank, it's pretty amazing what it will do for you. Every six months or so, ask for an increase on your credit card limit and on your line of credit. Each small increment is worth something.

SBA Loans. The Small Business Administration has a decent Web site at www.sba.gov. Their loans are federally guaranteed by the government and must be repaid. The lender is insured against a total loss, typically receiving 75 percent of the loan amount even if the borrower defaults. Therefore, banks are more likely to do riskier deals, which is good news for businesses with fewer than three years of operation.

SBA loans have eligibility guidelines. For instance, your company has to be profit making, operate in the United States, and be majority owned by a U.S. citizen or permanent resident. The SBA will consider your cash flow, detailed business plan including your exit strategy, two-year detailed monthly financial projections, an upward trend of your business, and past tax returns.

Every year the SBA will want to see improved revenues and decreased debt. If revenues are cyclical, that's okay, as long as it can see that your expenses have taken into account revenue fluctuations and profitability targets remain stable. The bottom line is, if you have cash flow and assets for collateral, you'll likely get a loan from the SBA. If not, it probably won't take the risk. Again, this is yet another reason to have a solid relationship with your banker, who will help you fill out the extensive SBA loan paperwork and will be a co-lender too.

GOVERNMENT GRANTS

Upside: It's free money!
Downside: There's government bureaucracy.

There are many types of government grants for small business innovation and research. The best thing to do is to check out www.grants.gov to learn more about grants for which you might be eligible. I'll just mention a few programs where you might start.

The SBIR is the Small Business Innovation Research program. This program helps fund small businesses in research and development efforts that have potential for commercialization. I know one entrepreneur who received over $1 million from the National Institutes of Health (NIH) under this program, and she claims that it wasn't hard to go through the process. Her company secured an SBIR Phase I grant for $150,000 to allow it to prove that its product would work in principle. Then it received a Phase II grant for $1 million for product development. This grant helped the company to attract financing from venture capitalists. Another entrepreneur launched a company to help the hearing impaired. He received $6 million in both government grants and direct funding from the Army—and he retained 100 percent ownership of his company, too.

Other programs include the Small Business Technology Transfer Program (STTR), offered through the NIH, and programs offered via universities. For example, the University of California has a BioSTAR grant program, which doubles the money an entrepreneur receives for a project.

Government grants are a huge topic, and I can't do them justice here. The net-net is that you can get millions of dollars that you'll never have to pay back if you can endure the excessive bureaucracy. Each grant will take about a year to write, submit, get approved, and get funded. If you have the patience, though, you'll not only get "free" dollars, but credibility and a prefab customer (the government) that will help you to attract additional types of capital in the future. Know the facts before you accept any type of grant; in some cases the sponsor may insist on owning the intellectual property you develop. Why give away the rights to your company's product? They're likely your greatest asset. Research the best type of grant for your needs before you dive in.

PERSONAL LOANS, UNSECURED LOANS, MICROLOANS, MERCHANT CASH ADVANCES, AND ASSET-BASED LENDING

Upside: They are easy to get; it's fast cash.
Downside: Many have high interest rates; personal loans carry relationship risks.

Personal Loans. Approximately $100 billion is informally invested in start-ups each year. Friends and family members alone provide over $60 billion, according to Babson College's studies on entrepreneurship. The key here is to have a formal financing agreement drawn up by an attorney, which makes it clear as to whether the financing is a loan, an equity investment, or a gift. For a loan, the agreement will state the interest rate and payment terms; for an equity investment, the percentage of ownership in the start-up. If the start-up succeeds and is sold or taken public, the equity investor can rest assured that it will be compensated. If the start-up fails, the lender-investor can write off the loss against its taxes.

Unsecured Loans and Microloans. I know of three great resources for unsecured business loans. TheSNAPloan .com provides business loans based on stated income, credit score, debt-to-income ratio, and years in business. Prosper.com also provides unsecured loans based on credit score and debt-to-income ratio, except their loans are provided by individuals and based on an auction model. Another site, Count-me-in.org, offers unsecured microloans as well, but for women-run businesses only.

Merchant Cash Advances. This type of financing is also called *credit card receivable funding.* Companies providing this service pay cash advances to businesses that meet certain qualifications based on their credit card sales history. The businesses then repay the advance, plus a premium, via deductions on future credit card sales. The advantage is that the business receives cash quickly without having to put up any collateral. The disadvantage is that this industry is not well regulated, so fees can be high. But you may choose this option if you aren't able to secure other funding sources. Check out www.advanceme.com.

Asset-Based Lending. This type of financing provides lending against accounts receivable via a traditional line of credit or factoring. With the traditional line of credit, the lender will review your accounts receivable and offer a credit line with an interest rate similar to a bank loan. With factoring, the lender will loan against an individual invoice. The lender may prefer a combination of purchase orders and invoices, since purchase orders state an *intention* to buy and invoices are issued when the sale is *completed.* For purchase order financing, the lender will likely offer 50 to 60 percent of the amount of a purchase order, and you'll have to prove that purchase orders ultimately become invoices.

With Kuvera, after maxing out my credit cards—and paying 20 percent interest —I discovered factoring, which only charged 5 percent interest. I used factoring to manage cash flow at both Kuvera and in the early days of Corporate Computing. The key is to consider the fee. If you're paying a 5 percent interest rate to the factoring company, you may want to offer your customers a discount on their invoices as an alternative. Think about it: if your customer agrees to pay in ten days in exchange for receiving a 2 percent discount on its invoice, you've saved the 3 percent difference you would have paid to the factoring company, assuming a 5 percent interest rate. And the savings are passed on to your customer. The only issue here is whether you can wait ten or more days to be paid.

Equipment Lease Lines

Upside: Rapidly depreciating items are used as collateral.
Downside: They can be hard to get or have heinous terms.

It often makes a lot of sense to lease computer hardware, cars, and software—things that lose their value quickly and have a high initial cost. A lease line enables you to buy the business equipment you need, using your purchases as collateral for this type of credit line. Do a Web search for equipment lease lenders in your community and ask your banker if they also provide lease lines.

Whew! Let's take a deep breath and move on to equity-based financing, where we'll consider two types: venture capital and angel financing.

Venture Capital

Upside: Financiers are sophisticated and have lots of money.
Downside: Only some will add value; you'll lose some
  control; they can fire you.

Venture capital (VC) is money provided by professionals who invest in rapidly growing start-up companies with the potential to develop into significant businesses. Professionally managed VC firms generally are private partnerships or closely held corporations whose funds can come from a variety of sources: private and public pension funds, endowment funds, foundations, corporations, and to a lesser degree, wealthy individuals, foreign investors, and the VCs themselves. VCs generally play many roles, including seeking companies to invest in, assisting in the development of new products or services for their portfolio companies, and adding value to those companies through active board participation. They take high risks by investing in ventures that haven't yet demonstrated success with the hope they'll provide high returns. They typically have a very long term view. The harsh reality is that VCs assume that most start-ups will fail.

VCs carefully evaluate and screen both the technical and the business merits of the company. During this due diligence process, the VC will conduct research on the market potential, competition, references, financial analysis, and product assessment. Commercial, legal, and personal aspects of the company will be considered, too. Your killer business plan should supply them with this information. VC financing is very tough to get, and not necessary to build a strong business. That said, many breakthrough businesses have been funded by VCs, including Apple, FedEx, Intel, Microsoft, eBay, and Google.

Angel Investment

*Upside: Increasing amounts are available; the money has
    fewer strings attached.*
*Downside: The sophistication and contributions of investors
    vary widely.*

Angel investors are high net worth individuals who may
or may not be savvy in your particular product or industry. "Friends and family" investments can be considered "angel financing." Angel investors may have a
similar investment philosophy to VCs. They often believe in the entrepreneur more than the actual product,
so they place their bet on the person with the compelling idea. Investment may take the form of a loan
that converts to stock, or preferred stock, or convert-
ible bonds. Rarely will the investment be in exchange
for common stock.

The Equity-Based Approach with
Institutional Investors

Each round of financing should be large enough to last
12 months or so. Most companies do three to five financing rounds prior to exit (such as a public offering
or being acquired by another company). The first, or
seed, financing round is a smallish one—a few hundred
thousand from friends, family, or angel investors. The
goal here is to prove your idea and develop a basic
product. Next is a more formal financing round, often

multimillions, with institutional investors such as banks or venture capitalists. Then comes round three, perhaps with corporate investors (such as a company strategic to a start-up's success) in addition to institutional investors. Around the third round the exit for the company is discussed. A fourth and sometimes fifth round of money may be raised in a manner similar to the third (though an investment banker may join the fray) prior to exit.

The Equity-Based Approach with Individual Investors

This is similar to the above, except with angel investors instead of institutional ones. You still need the right corporate structure (a C corporation, which can issue different classes of stock) and you'll have the ups and downs that accompany outside ownership. Investors invest to make money, so they'll eventually want to get their money out of your firm at the highest return possible. This changes the course of a company's growth. It accelerates it—a lot.

Regardless of which equity-based approach you take, you'll now have partners who can vote on company decisions, and sometimes your plans will be shot down. That said, it's often better than dangling alone on the financial hook. With equity the company's assets are at stake; with a secured loan, your personal ones are; with an unsecured loan no assets are at stake but the interest rate will be much higher.

The Loan-Based Approach

If you have a smaller business with fewer (initial) lofty goals and a more organic growth curve, a loan can be a good financing method. Loans generally come in the three flavors described above: Small Business Administration (SBA) loans, bank loans, or microloans. SBA loans are easier to get if you have assets to secure the loan, a solid pre-existing banking relationship, and a high tolerance for bureaucracy. If you make it through the process (I recommend a massive sense of humor), you can get a six- or seven-digit loan on pretty favorable terms. A bank loan often requires a pre-existing banking relationship. The terms will be based on your credit rating. A microloan will be smaller, and it will be unsecured. If you demonstrate goodwill with prompt payments, you'll be eligible for another larger loan in time.

Think hard about these issues during the financial planning stage. Get your executive team to agree on a common financing strategy so you don't have disagreement among the ranks midstream. Losing an executive mid-deal can destroy a financing. Once you and your team agree on the strategy and target, start knocking on those doors and testing out your financing pitch. Have a backup plan . . . plus a backup plan to your backup plan! Always work on multiple sources of financing and think of a consulting service you can provide for quick cash. Diversify with a blend of debt and equity. Always be in fund-raising mode: you can sometimes keep potential investors and financiers on the back burner for a future financing. Once you do all these things, you'll be well on your way to funding your company so you can achieve that next milestone.

YOUR COMPANY FINANCE CHECKLIST

1. *Create a capital acquisition strategy.* This is the four-step planning process explained above. This is the time to get a solid start-up-savvy attorney if you haven't yet!

2. *Contact the targeted financiers.* Start with the top five of the ten you put on your list. These should be financiers that match your industry, market, and stage of financing needed. If you are seeking venture capital money, most VC firms focus on a particular stage of investments—for example, Seed and Early Stage, Later Stage, or Mezzanine (pre-IPO). If you can, get a personal introduction from a friend who knows someone at the financier's firm. This will increase your chances of being moved to the top of the stack. Investors receive hundreds of business plans per month, and those that are not introduced personally have little chance of getting funded.

3. *The initial meeting.* Use your financing pitch presentation described in Chapter 3. If the financiers are interested and request it, give them your executive

(continues)

summary. Don't set a price for your company's equity—keep quiet. Let the investor tell you what he or she thinks it is worth.

4. *Follow-up.* If the financiers are still interested after reviewing your executive summary, they'll schedule another meeting with more members of their investment group. If that goes well, hand over your business plan. Never mail your business plan to an investor you have not yet met with. Spreading your plan around invites unwanted competition. Number each plan uniquely in the page footer. Track each copy. In the event your plan gets copied, you'll know who the culprit was.

5. *Secure a lead financier.* This financier does most or all of the due diligence, as well as helps bring other financiers into the deal. The lead drives the process—so get one pronto. The lead can be an angel investor or angel group, a VC, or a bank in the event that the financing you are doing is a loan. If you are getting a loan, you may not have other financiers.

6. *Set the stock price.* This step is only necessary for equity investors, which means angels and VCs. Setting the stock price occurs through negotiation with the investor and will be outlined in what's called the *term sheet*, which details the terms of the financing. Investors typically take preferred stock because it comes with certain rights and "preferences" that the

common stock does not, and they pay a higher price for it. Preferred stock might start out at something like $1 per share, whereas common stock will be about 10 percent of this price. Common stock is what will be divvied up among the rest of the folks, including your employees. Founders stock (or "sweat equity") is often one cent or so per share. Get help from your start-up-savvy attorney in setting the stock price, negotiating an employment agreement and stock option vesting schedule, among other things. Your CFO or controller should also be knowledgeable about start-up financing structures. It's easy to find an interim or part-time CFO or controller. Local accounting firms are often able to provide interim financial executives to small businesses.

7. *Paper the deal.* In this step, your attorney "papers" the deal with the appropriate legal contracts, which are executed by both parties. After this happens, the wire transfer is sent and you are funded. Now the work *really* begins.

COOL FREE RESOURCES

Go to www.RulesForRenegades.com and download "Setting Up Your Finance Department," "Effective Board Reporting," "Due Diligence Checklist," "Sample Term Sheet," "ROI-Focused Sales," "Personal Finance Checklist," and "The Value of Founder's Stock."

Resign as General Manager of the Universe

The Control Freak 12-Step Program

There must be more to life than having everything.

MAURICE SENDAK

HAVE YOU EVER BEEN burned out? If not, read this chapter as a cautionary tale. If so, you know how it happens. Burnout is insidious, as it is often born of success. You're so good at something that you are repeatedly offered opportunities to contribute more. And in the beginning, there's an intoxicating adrenaline buzz about it. You're achieving, you're being acknowledged for it, it feels good, and so you ratchet it up and accelerate the cycle. Externally everything looks peachy. Then you start to get a crazed look in your eyes. Your spouse, partner, or dear friend expresses concern. "Slow down," they say, "Rome wasn't built in a day." You begin to skip social activities; perhaps your love relationship starts to suffer. You're too damn busy for these things, and now's your moment, and it may never come again, so better grab that brass ring and rock 'n' roll.

But in your quiet times at the end of the day, when the adrenaline buzz wears off, you're just plain tired. And are you even feeling fulfilled? Honestly, is this how you want to live? Even when you think you have it all under control—the business, the personal life, and so on—there's always room for improvement. And sometimes improvement means slowing down.

Here's how I started to cop to my burnout.

It's Saturday. Or is it Friday? No, I'm pretty sure it's Saturday. My client meeting isn't until lunch, which means I practically have a day off. I drag myself out of bed, squish my feet into the hotel slippers, and pad into the bathroom. Looking in the mirror I see tired, lifeless eyes. Tons of gray hair—when did that happen? Aren't I paying someone to take care of that? Body: thin, but flabby. Face: sharp, let's-get-to-the-bottom-line expression. No softness, no tenderness. Bulging bags of excess skin rest under my eyes, my cheeks are sallow, sagging. I'm 34, but I don't look a day over 50.

If it's Saturday, then I must be in . . . actually, I have no freakin' idea what city I'm in. I grab the hotel room phone to search for clues. Hmmm . . . 214 area code. Texas? I ring the front desk.

"Front desk, may ah help yew?"

"Yes, please. What city am I in?"

"Why, yer in Dallas, Texas, sugar! Want some coffee sent up?"

"More than you know. Thanks."

What do normal people do on weekends? Go to the supermarket? I haven't been to one in years. My assistant says they sell juice in bags now—and low-fat Entenmann's pastries, and a zillion flavors of iced tea.

My friends have become so frustrated from so many unreturned calls that they've stopped leaving messages. I spend Sundays flying to wherever Monday's meeting takes place. My secretary has hired someone to run my household, fetch my dry cleaning, feed and walk my dogs. Pretty soon she'll be hiring someone to love and pet them. Oops. Guess she already did.

Whining, Dining, Resigning, or Time for Atlas to Shrug

Business has been booming for years. It's 1998, I think, and I've made it in the heady world of technology in my own right. Rama has long since faded into the woodwork. Bill Gates and I exchange friendly e-mails and talk shop. Complete strangers are sending me gifts and marriage proposals. I'm a parallel entrepreneur, launching up to six businesses at a time. Every day I'm in a different city, pitching clients, making speeches at $20,000 a pop, giving interviews to the business press. I've started companies, raised hundreds of millions of dollars, and made a few million for myself.

Then I get an e-mail that stops me dead in my Prada pumps.

> Resign as the General Manager of
> the Universe.

This is the message on my quote-of-the-day e-mail from BeliefNet.com. Resign? What a cop-out. General Manager of the Universe? Geez, that gig would require some epic control issues. I'm simply trying to make CEOs do what I want for their own good. I'm just trying to train my staff to do what I want, also for their own good. I'm only trying to convince the guy I'm dating to do what I want, yes, you've got it: for his own good. Why doesn't everyone simply *obey me*? Don't they understand that I know what's best for them? I need someone to help me get the people in my life in line. Hmmm. Maybe I need some help too.

I ask one of my mentors, Dr. Jerry Jampolsky, to dinner. He helped found the movement to help people convert fear to love with his bestselling book *Love Is Letting Go of Fear*. Jerry started the Center for Attitudinal Healing over 25 years ago, and now its 130 locations worldwide provide free support services for individuals and families dealing with life-threatening illnesses. Since control is about fear, I think he's the man to show my white-knuckling self how to loosen its grip.

We're at my favorite restaurant, but even though I missed lunch I have no appetite. Leaning forward, clutching the sides of the table, I say, "I feel so . . . God! So . . . *responsible*. Yeah, that's it. *Excessively* responsible." I slump back in my chair.

"Responsible for what?" Jerry asks, spinning the straw in his seltzer water, poking at the lemon wedge. He's always so mellow, so relaxed. Hey! I'm having a crisis over here. Listen up!

"*Everything*. Responsible for everything."

"Wow, that's a huge load to carry. Do you want to continue doing this?"

"No. I don't. But I have to do everything or it won't happen. I'm the only reliable one around here."

"Well, in that case, you can pay my mortgage," he winks.

"Not funny. Really, I need your help."

"Here," he says, digging in his jacket pocket. He pulls out a pad of paper and scribbles a prescription. He hands it to me. It says, "Spend one year not concerned with achieving anything."

"What does achievement have to do with control?"

"If you spent one year not concerned with achieving anything you'd understand."

And I try, honest I do. God knows I do. But I can't help myself. I achieve, and I'm concerned about it—I *need* to achieve. Achievement is what helps me know I matter, I have worth. But I overachieve and push myself to perform so hard that I no longer even feel my body—it becomes a liability, a limitation, something to rise above. But your body always gets revenge. It gets sick. It ages rapidly.

Four years later, I'm 38 and don't look a day over 60. Saggy jowls droop from my cheeks, dark deep pillows hang from below my eyes; I have paid the price for my workaholic ways. Yep, my body has won. Driving to a private clinic in San Francisco, I psych myself up for a "mini-lift." Ninety minutes from now the lower half of my face will be lifted, in a vain attempt to recapture some of my youth lost to workaholic ways.

I check my voice mail one last time before I go under the knife. Two of my co-investors want to renege on bridge loans. We'd all promised Company X a loan for six months to tide them over until their sales ramped up. Raising additional funds is nearly impossible since the Internet bubble burst, and my firm can't carry the load alone. The co-investors either need to fork over the cash or make the Call: "Merry Christmas! Your company is out of funding. Everyone's fired." It's too early to reach anyone, so I leave voice mail at each investor's office, asking them to do the right thing and keep their commitment. I realize then that I am always working. Always. And I resolve to change that. Like, *now*.

Over time I realized that I just couldn't hold it all together; my arms were overflowing with too many desperate attempts to control every aspect of my life. I wasn't even good at everything I was doing. At some things I was downright dreadful. But life is funny, isn't it? *The more you try to hold it all together, the more it has to fall apart. The more you try to control others, the more they shout, "Mutiny!" and jump ship.*

Burnout is directly proportional to being unwilling to delegate. Do you want to avoid burnout? Push more stuff off your plate and onto other people's plates. No, they won't do it the way you would. Maybe the outcome will be worse, but maybe it will be better. But the main thing is, you can't do everything. Believe me, I know this. I tried.

It's taken me decades to learn what I'm good at and what I'm lousy at. I'm a builder, not a long-term maintainer. I'm a marketer, not a manager, a salesperson, not a bean counter. I no longer regard it as a character flaw that I love to start businesses but want out after three to five years. I even tell everyone that up front. I have few employees and use contractors when I need extra help. Troubleshooting and providing solutions are strengths of mine, but that doesn't mean I have to stick around and execute every idea. I accept now that I often prefer solitude to socializing and that socializing is fun for the first few hours but can become exhausting.

It took me years to figure out how my brain worked, what I was born to be good at, what I should avoid. Yes, when you finally discover what you're good at *and* enjoy, sometimes it takes guts to do it. Yes, it may not make you rich initially, but success isn't all about wealth. Too many people get stuck in a career that a high school counselor divined through those weird tests and said they had an aptitude for. Or found a summer job at McDonald's and wound up in the food service industry. Or maybe you were one of the lucky ones who found out early in life what you were good at *and* made you happy.

Whether you discovered your gifts—and your gaps— early or late, you'll want to have someone else to do the stuff you suck at. Flesh out your team with talent you don't have. This is tough when you're a control freak or are accustomed to being in charge, or when you think your way is the best way. But it's the only way to avoid burnout.

The Fish Rots at the Head

I wish I could say that whenever I grabbed the reins as CEO, I was a star performer, but as the Japanese say, "The fish rots at the head." If there's a problem with a company, look to the head of it: first the CEO, then the board of directors. Something's rotten. When you're in a difficult phase, when your life's not working, look inside. The head is what either hurts or heals, and it's up to you to foster the attitudes and thoughts that determine your desired outcome. Positive attitudes and thoughts energize you; negative ones do just the opposite. Isn't choice great?

When I did manage to turn over the reins, I made yet another set of mistakes. I repeatedly hired the wrong business partners and executives, and all for the same reason: fear. Fear of losing control. Fear of trusting others. Fear of failure. Fear always impairs judgment—especially in hiring decisions. Needless to say, these ill-fated partnerships didn't last long. At one company I was afraid I didn't have enough sales experience, so I hired an MBA. It turns out I did most of the selling anyway, so I ended up having to buy out my partner's share. I hadn't figured out my strengths yet, hadn't figured out my standards of the performance of others, either. When a control freak first experiments with delegation she'll likely make mistakes. She's learning a new behavior and has to course-correct as she goes. In time and with practice I made some exceptional hires who were highly accountable, constantly took the initiative, and cared about the company as much as I did.

At this point some self-reflection is required. *You are the only problem you'll ever have . . . and you're the solution, too.* When things are messed up or not going as smoothly as you'd like, do a self-assessment. List what you might be doing to cause your own problems, talk to a friend, and bounce your ideas off him or her; chances are good that you know what the problem and solution are already. Now it's time to take action and make some changes.

As a reforming control freak, I can now admit that I can't control people, situations, or outcomes. Sometimes, though, I can influence them. As a result, I find that I have far less stress in my life than before. I attract staff members who are more take-charge than before because they know I won't take charge for them. I have more realistic expectations of people's performance as well as when deadlines will *really* be achieved. As a control freak I set myself up for disappointment—I even *expected* it. As a person who is in control of only myself, I expect people to come through for me. And that's what I experience most often now. You will too, when you build a rockin' team.

In addition to your team, everyone needs one or more mentors to bounce ideas off, to shine light on our blind spots. If you're a CEO, you also need a strong advisory board of seasoned and successful executives. Hiring team members is one thing; bringing on a business partner is another. Don't take on a business partner until you've worked together at least six months and solved multiple business challenges. Have the "divorce" (severance) agreement inked and signed along with the "marriage" (hiring) agreement. Make sure the severance terms are spelled out in advance. The more often you have this, the less often you need it. If you find you're not good at hiring people (fess up, now!) have your advisor-mentor with the skill set you lack help you hire staff and monitor their work. And if a team member isn't working out, let him or her go quickly—because it only gets worse from there. Remember the golden rule of hiring: hire slowly, fire quickly.

Get Numb to Your "Number"

People talk about their "number"—the amount of money that will make then financially free, allow them to retire from the rat race. In Silicon Valley, we call it "F**k-You Money"—having enough to be able to say so long to any job. But what they don't talk about is the artificial inflation of that number from an excessive lifestyle. When you're on the workaholic more-more-more fast track, you often surround yourself with expensive luxuries in an attempt to feel better. Yes, you've "earned" these luxuries from all your hard work and sacrifices, but honestly, do they make your life better? Do they feed your soul? Didn't think so.

However, I know people who are driven to make more, not because they are fundamentally insecure, but simply because they like the rush. I've known a handful of people with a net worth of several hundred million dollars who look and act like an ordinary Joe on the street. They don't give a hoot about luxuries. And guess what? They're often the happier bunch. And most often they value relationships above everything else.

Toys are transitory. So is your number. Most of us start out in our careers focused on achieving goals, and after years of hard work and life experience some of us decide that what really matters is relationships, giving back, having fun in business, and not killing ourselves by always working insane hours.

Here's my net-net on control and burnout. Control freaks often burn out because they won't delegate. They don't trust that others will come through for them. They lack trust because they are disconnected from both themselves and others. They are disconnected because relationships haven't been a priority. So what matters is connection, because connection fosters trust.

Many of us sense this. But do we live by it? What will it take to make you wake up to it? I let myself get numb and number, building up my Rolodex, breaking down my deeper connections. My first wake-up call was in 1991, when I had a cancer scare. I realized I had no one to call, no one to help me through this experience. The loneliness and terror of being wheeled into the operating room, not sure what the doctor would say afterward, was overwhelming. Four years later, I had a second cancer scare. My doctors told me that my body was sending me a message, but I couldn't slow down, wouldn't slow down. I had lots of other body-oriented wake-up calls. My dentist told me I'd need massive dental reconstruction because I ground my teeth so violently in my sleep—but I didn't even notice the problem until I saw my slanted smile in my wedding photos.

What Loyalty Looks Like

But when someone else's mortality—someone I thought would never wither and die—slapped me in the face, it was finally time to pay attention. This wake-up call was piercingly loud.

"There's a 20 percent chance he'll make it to Christmas," Dr. Stein tells us. It's October 2003.

Nine months earlier my father was a tall, dark, tribal chieftain of a man: proud and courageous, the friend people turned to for leadership and solutions in times of trouble. Descended from the Black Irish, his last name, Comaford, was derived from "common fort," where the warriors would gather prior to joining a battle. The oncologist, surgeon, and gastrointestinal specialist all say the same thing: Dad has pancreatic cancer, stage four. There is no stage five.

By mid-December the cancer has worn Dad down, slowly at first, then devouring him these past two months in a sadistic sprint. His face is sunken, his 6-foot, 3-inch frame is all bone with just a little flesh and muscle hanging on.

Shortly before the diagnosis, I'd merged my VC fund and was transitioning into an advisory role. I'd been seeking a slower, more sane pace, breathing a lot more, controlling a lot less. Upon Dad's diagnosis I pronounce myself officially retired. Faced with his loss, I suddenly realize how much he matters to me, and how little I know him. I have the chance to find out who he is and I'm not going to blow it.

After 30 years of an incredibly fractious, complicated relationship, my father and I become close confidants. Over his last months, we relive our arguments and amnesties and forgive each other. Dad tells me what I've yearned to hear: that I was always okay in his eyes, even if I wasn't a boy. I'm just what he wanted. Didn't I know that from the nickname he'd given me? "Tiger Baby" is the name of a warrior, one who always lands on her feet, rises up, and finds her way.

Dad asks me to make three promises: to look after Mom and help her through his death, to encourage her to remarry, and to scatter his ashes in the sea behind Kimo's, his favorite Maui burger joint. I promise.

A few days later, his breathing is more labored. He finds it difficult to speak, has refused medication and his favorite strawberry protein shake, and has barely sipped water. His body is shutting down. I try to smile when I tell him I love him, in those long hours when I look after him while my mother rests or goes to the pharmacy. Holding my tears inside requires a level of discipline I don't think I have. I finally give up, and let myself cry in front of him. Just little tears, not the gut-wrenching sobbing I do under the covers in the guest bedroom alone at night.

My mother sleeps on the thin pad from the patio's chaise lounge at the foot of Dad's sick bed. She's slept there for the past few weeks so she can hear his faintest groan, be at his side instantly if he needs her. I stare at the thin mattress. *This is what loyalty looks like. Look. Look at it. Remember it. Etch it on your mind. This is what you want to be for others, and for others to be for you.*

My mother had looked away for years. She looked away when Dad came home from his "business dinners" at 5 a.m. She looked away when I found the pearl-drop earrings in Dad's car—earrings that weren't hers, my sister's, or mine. She looked away when I answered the phone calls from unfamiliar women asking if Dad was home. Finally she stopped looking away. She and I left him when I was 16 years old. We drove across the country, from Connecticut to California, each in a different car. Yes, we took Dad's gold Mercedes.

Out west we started our lives over, as we had when I was 14 and my parents first separated. I hated my father. It was a potent hate, the kind only love can fuel.

Thirteen years after their divorce was final, my parents remarried. He'd learned what he had lost, and she'd regained her self-respect. This new marriage had rules though, and fidelity was the first one. I cried throughout the intimate ceremony, seeing for the first time an expression of deep devotion on my father's face. Such love, such total adoration. I was 34.

Dad had never been much of a hand holder when I was young, but now we hold hands often. His strong hands have turned into soft, tender sausages swollen from prednisone, then morphine. Those hands in mine say *I'm sorry, I've made a mess of things,* then later, as the cancer progresses, *Please forgive me.*

I do, my hands reply. *Forgive me too?* My hands ask, gently stroking his.

Yes, his hands squeeze back.

December 23. Dad is still holding on. I know he'll push to make it two more days just to beat the odds and prove the doctor wrong. He's the sort of man who always defies statistics. I sit by his bed, stroking his hands, and lean close to hear his whisper.

"Love you, Tiger Baby."

"Love you, Daddio."

He's half there, half somewhere else. He points around the room, acknowledging visitors I can't see. Are loved ones appearing to show him the way to the next world? He seems surprised that so many "escorts" have come for him. I sense his father, his mother, his stepmother, and many others I don't know.

It's 4 a.m. when Mom and I finally go to sleep. When I kiss my father goodnight, his eyes are staring off into the distance.

When I wake up three hours later, he's gone. It's December 24.

———————

Spending those last 11 months with my father was the hardest and most sacred work of my life, and I feel lucky ten thousand times over for the privilege of doing it. I've never felt more strongly that this was one of my life's key lessons:

Forgive the one who has hurt you most.

He shaped my life, he started me running from myself at age seven, but I was his willing accomplice. My feet ran, but no one forced them except me. And then exactly as he had started me on this path, he helped me come full circle at age 41.

How Connected Are You?

In the process of grieving my father's death, I thought about connection a lot. How many meaningful relationships did I have in my life? How many groups did I love and had I become active in? How many people did I appreciate daily?

When I met my husband, Chris—the man who saw my photo in the *Fortune* magazine spread and got in touch—I was amazed at how connected he was with his family, how much time he spent visiting them, talking on the phone, sending cards. When I met them, I was overwhelmed by the feeling of being in the presence of a tight-knit tribe, of people who forgave one another, helped one another, accepted one another with all their flaws. I'd told my friends I'd never get married or have kids. Then I met this fascinating man and pow! We married two years later and I became the step-mom to a sweet seven-year-old boy. Nothing in my childhood or adult life prepared me to be a parent. I devoured books on step-parenting, talked to a family therapist, and nervously entered the deep end of the parenting pool. Joining my husband's family, getting closer to my mother as a result of helping her through Dad's illness, caring for a child—all changed my life in ways building businesses and achieving worldly ambitions never could.

I finally started to study—yes, I was that clueless—how to connect with people, my community, my family, my in-laws. I modeled how my husband stayed in touch with others, sent cards, called for no apparent reason. How he pulled people together socially. I'd done that too, but I'd become overfocused on pulling people together to network, to further their careers, or to support nonprofits as opposed to just getting together to connect with no other agenda. When I was younger, I wanted to be a star. And I became one. I also ran my health into the ground and completely lost sight of the importance of connection. Now I'm more interested in helping others birth their businesses. I'm a starmaker, not a star.

Until I resigned as the General Manager of the Universe I was stuck in the control freak cycle, which led to burnout. Then life forced me to learn to let go. But the best part is that the more you give others a chance to rise up and be reliable, the more accountable they will be. And the more you value them, the greater connection you'll build, which will increase their desire to come through for you.

THE SEMI-ANNUAL ASSESSMENT

It's essential to assess where you are in your life; otherwise, one or both of the following will happen. First, you could wake up years later miles downstream from where you planned. Second, you won't get the hang of letting go, which is essential in order to avoid burnout. Here's how to do it: Twice a year (I like June and December), take yourself away from it all. If you can afford it, go away by yourself. If you can't, lock the bathroom door. Then ask yourself these questions:

- Is my personal life working?

  - Am I progressing in my self-discovery/spirituality?

  - Am I feeling close to God, or am I getting too swept up in stuff?

  - Am I my best friend; do I love myself?

  - Am I being honest with myself and others—authentic and not fake or defensive?

  - Am I stretching enough outside of my comfort zone?

  - What am I still afraid of?

  - Where can I go and what can I do to get to the next level?

  - Are my relationships deeply fulfilling?

- Is my career working?

  - Am I learning, stretching, challenging myself?

  - Am I building my network of fascinating people by at least five people per month?

  - Am I being honest with myself and others—authentic and not defensive?

(continues)

- What am I still afraid of?

- Where can I go and what can I do to get to the next level?

- Are my relationships deeply fulfilling?

- Am I becoming a more integrated human being, bringing my spirituality into the way I interact with others, being okay with who I am, taking care of myself?

- Am I copping to the fact that I'm the only problem I'll ever have—and I'm the solution too?

- Am I accepting people exactly as they are, not expecting them to change? If certain people in my work or personal life are challenging to me, am I willing to accept that that's just how they are? (See Chapter 2, pp. 39-40.)

- Am I being patient with the changes that take time? Am I appreciating all I have? Am I tolerant of those with different struggles?

- Am I achieving my goals in all these seven areas: financial and wealth, career, free time/fun, health and appearance, relationships, personal development, community and charity?

- Am I connected to all the important sides of my life (personal, family, intellectual, spiritual, recreational)?

COOL FREE RESOURCES

Go to www.RulesForRenegades.com and download "Seeking Balance via Connection," "Future Planning Worksheet," "Goal Setting Worksheet," "How to Create an Advisory Board," "Effective Board Reporting," and "Making Decisions based on ROI."

Don't Just Do Something, Stand There

Meeting a Corpse at the L.A. County Morgue and Learning the Secret to Life

We should give as we would receive, cheerfully, quickly, and without hesitation; for there is no grace in a benefit that sticks to the fingers.

SENECA

TO PERSEVERE in the face of overwhelming odds, you first need the inner strength that comes from knowing that no matter what happens, you'll still have *you*. For this you have to locate your unshakable core, you have to decide what your boundaries are, what you will and won't put up with, what your source of inner strength is.

In a perfect world, we'd have teachers and mentors who would help us figure out what we believe in, what we stand for, while we're still in our teens and twenties—while we're getting bombarded with social pressures and before we get caught up in the hurly-burly of shaping our career, creating our life, and stamping out fires. Without that kind of foundation, it's easy to get lost and stay lost. Getting to know yourself, of course, is a life-long process, but why not learn what you can sooner than later?

It took me a while to get to it, but here's my philosophy in a nutshell: I believe in karma. Whatever you do and whatever you think will come back to you, for good or ill. When you make a mistake, you can clean it up right away, or you do it later when everything's crusty and dried hard onto the counter. So you might as well clean it up now. I believe that since the world is moving faster and faster, we're seeing a lot more "instant karma." Do something funky, and it'll come back to you *faster* than before. If we follow this simple code—simple to understand, not always simple to follow—we'll be happier and experience more peace.

Remembering and Forgetting

Life is a cycle of remembering and forgetting. When we remember what matters most, we're happy, aligned with our life purpose, and everything's rosy. Then we forget. We're confused, scared, angry, and ego driven, and we wonder why life sucks so completely. Sooner or later we'll remember, and our suffering ends—until we forget again. It's taken decades for me to understand this, to have compassion with myself and others when we're in our "forgetting" phases, to recognize when I'm lost and to use the tools I have to find myself again. But the more I witness this phenomenon, the more it rings true.

I've been interested in self-discovery and spirituality for as long as I can remember. At 13, I began reading books to figure out why there was so much suffering in the world, and what I could do about it. The ones on Buddhism struck a gong in me. At 17, I took the next step and became a monk. A few years later, I'd forgotten why, and as I mentioned in Chapter 7, Rama sent me to a morgue with a forensic pathologist whose job was to help me remember.

———————

"Y ou've meditated in graveyards, right?" Dr. Ilene Patterson shuffles up to me after meditation class one day. She peers a little too close into my face. "Graveyards. You've meditated in 'em, right?"

"Yeah. Bunch of times. No biggie." *Duh. Like, I'm a Buddhist monk. Graveyard meditation is Exploring Mortality 101: Basic Buddhism.*

I took my vows three years ago, but some of my fellow monks say I'm not getting it, say I act like I'll live forever. It's all part of the Spiritual Sweepstakes. Some of the grouchy older monks try to psych out the spunky new ones, as if there's not enough enlightenment to go around. Whatever.

"All right, let's see how tough you really are. We're going to the L.A. County Morgue. Meet me in the parking lot at 1140 North Mission Road. Saturday. 10:00 a.m."

"Okay, I'll be there."

"You bet you will."

I will. I will? Ilene knows what she's doing. I mean, she's a monk and all. She took her vows when she was really old, like 40 or something. She's a grown-up Buddhist. I'm a baby Buddhist, 20 years old. Babies—they have such huge egos. And according to Ilene, everyone in the Malibu ashram is sick of mine. Yeah, well I'm sick of some stuff too. I mean, I've taken my vows, and I'm not getting laid, but I'm not getting enlightened either. So what's the deal?

Rama thinks we should live and work in the world with our monastic vows intact. He's ordered Ilene to help me understand this impermanence thing, that nothing lasts, least of all our bodies. And I've got one buff body. Buff. I'm a member of Pete's Butt Busters at the Sports Connection gym in West Hollywood.

When I first learned what Ilene was, what she does, I was kind of freaked out. She looks like a vulture—stubby square body, sharp beaked nose, high hunched shoulders. Can you imagine her crouching over corpses, cutting up dead bodies, doing the gritty, grisly work of the autopsy? It's not a job I could do, but it seems to suit her fine.

It's a warm Saturday as I drive east on Sunset. The fog is just lifting. I pull my VW Rabbit into the parking lot. Ilene zooms past in her Fiat Spider. Screechy violin music blares as she cuts the engine, clambers out of her car, and swivels over to me on short vulture legs. She's looking through those glasses of hers, the ones that get darker outside. They're pretty dark inside, too.

"Ready?"

"Sure, let's go."

"We're gonna go all right. And you're gonna see things you'll never forget. Never. And I'm gonna show 'em to you." Ilene walks ahead, leads me to a thick gray door. It squeaks open, thunks closed.

"Welcome," she hurls over her sloped shoulder, "to the L.A. County Morgue."

Bodies. Bodies everywhere. They're on gurneys two rows deep. They're under those lumpy sheets. I can't see them, but I know they're there. They're there. The smell betrays them—the syrupy stench of nose-piercing chemicals coupled with fusty flesh. I breathe through my mouth, but can't shut the odor out. This version of death is 3-D, not like the photos of cadavers we monks meditate on. This version is in-your-face, all over your senses.

"Hey, Ilene?" I whisper, "people must be dying all over the place, all the time."

"Yeah, people have a way of doing that."

"Yeah?"

"Yeah. They do it so often we're running out of room. For Chrissakes, stop whispering. It's not like you're gonna wake anybody up." *Ree-e, ree-e, ree-e,* Ilene rolls a gurney to the right, peels back the sheet on a 30-something Latino man. Dark curls frame his face and fall onto the gurney's cool silver surface, his tight waxy skin glows yellow under the fluorescent lights. She opens the door. "We'll see to him later."

"Um, Ilene?"

"Yeah? What now?"

"How did he die?"

"Hit by a car on the 405. Take note—don't walk down the middle of the freeway. Could shorten your life expectancy."

"Has he, uh, been here long?"

"Well, take a good look," She nudges me closer. "What do you think?"

"Um, I dunno." He's a close imitation of life. Like a mannequin in a store window you glimpse at as you walk by, and you swear you saw it breathe and twitch so you stop, look, and the life's been snatched right out of it. You're standing there on the sidewalk staring at it with a twisted feeling in your gut, wondering if you imagined that sparkle in its eyes. "I've, um, never seen a dead body before. Never been to a funeral."

"Funeral's later. Autopsy's first. His is in about an hour."

"Autopsy?"

"Sure. You've seen him on the outside. May as well see him on the inside."

My gut gurgles—loud. *I'll barf, I just know I'll barf when she cuts him open.*

"C'mon. We're going to the fridge."

"Oh, boy, I don't think I could eat right now . . ."

"Good. 'Cause you aren't gonna wanna eat there." Ilene opens the solid steel door with a click and a whoosh. We step in. It thunks closed behind us.

"This is the fridge, where we store the corpses."

Dang, it's cold in here. Chilly bumps crawl up my legs. I didn't realize I'd be in a giant refrigerator. This pink flowered tank top and matching shorts don't cover much.

Ilene leads me from the shallow entry into a room brimming with bare bodies. My legs stop, muscles stiffen, and throat squeezes. No sheets here. No hiding, no hinting at death. These are stacks, *racks* of women. They're piled six high on metal trays like loaves of bread at the bakery. But they're not warm and aromatic; they're cold, odorless. They line the walls and fill the room, creating a maze of trays. The air is thick with souls of the freshly dead.

"Okay, I got you here. Now you're on your own." Click. Thunk. Ilene's gone. She's coming back, though. Right?

Well I'm not staying in here alone. Like, forget it. I grab the door handle, yank hard. *Gotta . . . get . . . this . . . stupid . . . door . . . open. Whoooo! It's stuck. Okay, don't freak out. Breeeeathe. Geez, it's cold in here. Feel so naked . . . just like these bodies all around me, all waiting to be cut or to be claimed. They could be sleeping, dreaming. In their twenties, thirties, dreaming they're tall, thin, desirable. And they are, they actually are. Where are the old? Where are the ugly?*

I take a tiny step toward the racks, look down at a lean

brunette. Overhead the light flickers, lends her a greenish glow. God, she's about my age. Long face, thin lips, wavy hair pools on the tray behind her olive-skinned-back. God, she kinda looks—*looked*—like me. Now her skin's chalky, her lips pale, her hair brittle. What happened to her? How did she die? Drunk? Drugged? Driving? Where was she going? To work? To workout?

Surely she hadn't entered the warm L.A. day feeling, knowing, she'd be dead by dusk, in the fridge by sunset, in the graveyard tomorrow. Surely she hadn't felt, hadn't known that some stranger, me, would be staring at her asking such questions. I want to touch this brunette, see if she is as solid, rigid, and, well, *dead* as she seems. But I can't move. Stiff. Stuck. Glued on the gray linoleum floor.

Okay, do it. Be brave. Face scrunched up and body leaning back, I take a tiny step toward her tray. Stretching my arm forward, I tap hers and jerk back. Her arm's cold, green-apple hard. Touch my arm—warm, pliable, a peach in its prime. I step closer. Touch her. Touch me. Her. Me.

My heart feels like it's busting open, and I slump to the floor. Sorrow slashes the center of my chest—sorrow for her, sorrow for me, sorrow for everyone, everything that will one day perish. No more arm's-length now. We're too close for that.

On my knees now, chest heaving, I look at her face: beautiful and blank. I reach out, take her lifeless hand in mine, squeeze it, hold it. Who was she? Was she well loved? Did she love well? Am I? Do I?

Life. So precious. So perfect. So fleeting, like the salty tear sliding down my cheek. I catch it with my tongue, taste it, smell it. Sweet and bitter, fragrant and fetid, a concerto and the clanging of tin, tray upon tray. On the floor of the fridge, surrounded by the dead, holding the hand of a corpse, I remember why I became a monk in the first place: to help people, to reduce human suffering. I return the woman's hand, rest it on her tray, slide it beside her thigh. *Thank you. Thanks.*

Rising, I wobble to the door, turn the handle, stagger out of the fridge. I stumble down the gray tile hall, one hand on the off-white wall as tears splash my pink flowered tank. My legs collapse out the side door, out to the pavement of the parking lot, into the clear late afternoon.

And I head west. West on Sunset.

———————

The woman—the corpse—reminded of so many things. First, that one day I'd die, and it might be sooner than I thought . . . so it was time to get on with doing what mattered most to me. Second, that the whole reason I became a monk was to reduce human suffering—what was I doing about it lately? Not much. I had forgotten; I had lost my direction. It was time to assess my situation, to face what mattered in my life, to become who I needed to be.

But as they sometimes are, this was a partial remembering. Yes, I got more in touch with myself as a result of this experience, but still I thought someone else, Rama, was necessary to enable the realization of my goals. And the trouble with remembering is that sooner or later we'll forget again.

Find Your Groove

That particular remembering from the morgue lasted for four years. At age 24 the cloistered life wasn't fitting me anymore. We were all meditating to transcend human suffering, but I wanted to get down with it, roll around in it, be more hands-on. I broke my vows, got a burger and a boyfriend. By 29 I was knee-deep in the world of money. I figured maybe the answer was to make a bunch of dough—maybe money would help reduce human suffering. But in the hurly-burly of making my way in business, and after leaving Rama, I let go of much of my spiritual practice. I stopped meditating for seven years, tumultuous years when the bursting of the tech bubble caused thousands around me to lose their jobs and I had to counsel CEOs through difficult transitions—laying off staff, liquidating assets. Sheer will and perseverance got me through. Spirituality would have helped a lot more.

I don't want to put myself out there as this great example of spirituality, because I'm not. But I think I'm a decent example of the value of the quest. Whenever I got really stuck I would seek help. I walked on burning coals at a Tony Robbins seminar; I retreated to the desert and studied with a shaman; I did ropes courses, and meditated at assorted ashrams. My questing was inconsistent, and the results didn't last. Within weeks I'd be mired again in the mess of pushing too hard to succeed. By age 40, I knew it was time to slow down, reconnect with myself. And then my father was diagnosed with cancer.

What grand lesson did I finally learn from it all? That there is always going to be suffering, no matter how wholly I commit myself to ending it. But what else did I figure out? That I can make a difference, reducing it a little bit every day. Having a spiritual practice has helped me articulate and live my core values: a commitment to compassion and community as a fundamental part of any business or life plan.

My spiritual practice has helped me embrace another powerful core belief: people are fundamentally good. Actually, everyone is fundamentally fabulous; some of us just get confused along the way. It seems to me that people are coming from either love or fear. That's what I love about the human race; we're totally complex, but we're really simple at the same time. If someone's coming from love, I know that they'll want to help me and be supportive. If they're coming from fear, a lot of funky emotions will come up. When I hold onto that belief, it's easier for me to deal with people in a more compassionate, less knee-jerk way. I see that most of what comes across as anger and aggression is actually fear. Fear I can deal with. Remembering this helps me not take it so personally when someone is unkind to me.

Many people tell me they are seeking their purpose in life; they're waiting for that divine epiphany where their mission becomes blindingly clear. Until then they're in the grand "waiting room" of life—and let me tell you, there's a *huge* crowd in there. And it's OK to wait, to be still, to get clarity. Yes, the uncertainty may be excruciating. That's a good sign—keep still and the clarity will come. Just don't expect it to be delivered in a detailed divine message.

I don't receive divine messages that are complete and clear. I receive divine sticky notes. You've received these too. Maybe you had an insight as you were walking in nature, meditating, when your mind was still. Did you follow that message? Did you implement it in your life? I've found that when I do, it leads to more messages. Then months later I look back and marvel at what has come of that one tiny insight. The waiting room is a place of transition if you use it properly. To do so you need to simplify your life, to make space for what's coming. I do this after I exit each company I create or when a significant relationship ends. Suddenly there's a big gap in my life, and I have to breathe through the compulsion to fill it fast—to do anything but feel the emptiness. Breathe, be still, wait for a what's next. It *always* comes.

To increase my stillness, I meditate daily for about 30 minutes in the morning, with "spot checks" of a few minutes throughout the day when I need them. The vast majority of my business and technology innovations, company ideas, marketing plans, and life insights have come from the clarity I get when I stop my barrage of thoughts. Intuition follows from paying attention. Learn to pay attention, and you'll begin to hear the quiet voice within that will guide you.

Every ten weeks or so, I go on a retreat—just me, alone with (or without) my thoughts. Some retreats are silent, some aren't. I hike, spend time in nature, dream.

For days I'll just be by myself, recharging my batteries, perhaps focusing my attention on a single problem or issue I need help with.

I'm not advocating that you follow my spiritual path—or any spiritual path, for that matter. I do recommend embracing self-discovery, though. Find out what matters most to you, then gather the tools that will help you check in with yourself when you've drifted away from your unshakable core, lost sight of your most important goals.

You need a single set of ground rules for all the parts of your life. *One* set. Not "I'll be fabulous to everyone I love outside work, but I'll stab a co-worker in the back to get ahead." Your spiritual life isn't separate from the rest of your life. I'm an integrated human being, and I need an integrated approach to leading my life. I think we all do.

It's funny, but everyone spends so much time talking about work-life balance, and so little time talking about the need for a spiritual practice and service. I find those are the best ways for me to stay balanced. We're all busy, sure, but everyone can find one hour per week or a few hours per month to volunteer. Volunteering can bring you experiences that will shape your life in ways you couldn't possibly imagine.

"I love you," Charlotte wheezes.

"Um, I love you too." I mean, I guess I do. I only met Charlotte an hour ago. This intensity of emotion is startling. I guess when you're dying, you don't waste time.

I've become a volunteer for home- and hospital-bound patients with the Center for Attitudinal Healing. The combination of wanting to reduce human suffering plus the despair I'd felt after my two cancer scares drew me to this work. After six months of training, I'm ready to work with patients.

One of my first is Charlotte. She was born with cystic fibrosis, and at only 24 years of age breathing is a chore for her; she often hacks like a feeble old man. I will learn over the coming months that Charlotte is one of the kindest and happiest people I've ever met. "How lucky I am to have such a wonderful life," she says every time I visit. As her lips move, the ever-present oxygen tube in her nose bounces on her face, dividing it like a crack down the middle of a fragile porcelain vase.

Charlotte knows that her time is running out weeks before I do. Gulping shot glasses of liquid morphine, followed by cranberry juice chasers, she enlists me as her willing bartender in this macabre saloon. "I'm not ready . . . to leave everyone behind . . ." She pants after each phrase. Her lungs are filling up. This is how CF kills you: you suffocate. "I need . . . to get out. . . . Your house?"

"Yes, of course, we'll cook dinner—all your favorite foods. Let's see—lobster, asparagus, and chocolate cake with raspberries." I check an imaginary list on my palm, playing waitress. "Did I miss anything, ma'am?" Charlotte beams.

.   .   .

A week later Charlotte shuffles up to my front door at a speed of three feet per minute. Her husband carries her shrunken frame up the four stairs, but she insists on walking over the threshold. We feast and watch the sunset in silence, listening to the lapping of the tide against the rocks. Charlotte removes her oxygen tube, leans over the deck railing, and takes in deep, laboring breaths of salty air.

It's her last night out.

A few days later she goes into the hospital. I read poetry to her, and we talk about our lives and our loves. Charlotte begins dictating those long-delayed letters, saying goodbye to the people she cherishes. Even though her family is nearby, letters help her express the deep personal feelings that often choke her up, both emotionally and physically.

.   .   .

One night I'm at a launch party for one of my clients. I duck out of the noisy room to call Charlotte at the hospital, to wish her sweet dreams. "I can't wait to see you tomorrow, Charlotte. I have a gorgeous new poem for you."

"Won . . . der . . . ful," she gasps.

"See you tomorrow. Love you."

"Luh . . . vuh . . . you."

The phone rings the next morning; Charlotte died at 6:30 a.m. Why *this* morning? I still have so much to tell her, to share with her, to thank her for. I should have skipped that launch party, should have been at the hospital with her. After all those years in the fiercely competitive business world, Charlotte reminded me of the most important things in life: loving and caring for others. She also taught me how to breathe. How to feel the air in my lungs, how to be thankful for it.

―――――――――

My next hospice patient, Bob, teaches me to let go of anger, and to embrace forgiveness. Years later, volunteering at LifeWorks, an organization that helps abused children, teaches me how to reawaken struggling kids to love, attention, and consistency. Most of us come to volunteer work with the goal of giving. What we find, though, is that we receive so much more than we ever imagined.

You Don't Have to Be Good to Do Good

Volunteering is a vital part of my life now: hospice, addiction, literacy, entrepreneurship, the environment. I have a deep need to make a difference, yet it took me a while to build a consistent volunteering practice into my routine. Writing checks is easy, donating time is harder.

What took me so long? Will it take you that long? So often we want to do good, but we tell ourselves, "I'll give once I'm rich," or "I'm overwhelmed by all the causes, I'll give once I've had time to research them." Driving into Silicon Valley or any other emporium of the more-more-more mindset will convince you: You need a better car! You need a bigger house! You need to hoard your cash for *you*—why give to others? The result? We don't give anything, when even a little bit could really make a difference. What do you want your contribution to the world to be? What's your plan for leaving things just a little bit better than you found them?

Money and success are often distracting. That's why if you commit to giving back from the get-go, and build it into your life, you'll stay more grounded on your way to the big time. It works for me to make giving back as much a business decision as a personal life choice. If you decide that giving back is going to be one of your core values, you can plan around it. A while back I met some cool entrepreneurs of a Swiss start-up. They decided from the beginning that they were going to fund their company's business *and* a charitable foundation *simultaneously*—that way, their vision of service to others would be built into the very core of their company and the very core of their values. I'm *so* not a saint; sometimes I think that doing good is one of my most selfish acts. Heck, out of a desire to do some good I've had many amazing opportunities: I told you about my first date with Bill Gates and the invite to the White House, and that's just the beginning. If the perks of giving get you started, I say go for it. I'm betting that the satisfaction you feel from giving a part of yourself will keep you involved.

As I was writing this chapter I tried an experiment. I decided to volunteer with a nonprofit in an industry new to me where I wanted more contacts. The executive director asked me to do many challenging tasks to help his cause, and I willingly took them on. In exchange, he would connect me with the major players in this industry. Guess what happened? I worked my butt off, delivered terrific results, received zero introductions to industry players, and got resentful. The resentment and anger came from feeling ripped off. How about a little acknowledgment or appreciation for my considerable contributions? Nada. My ego was shrieking. Seeking to get unstuck, I called one of my mentors. He reminded me that "if only" is what egos say when they go to Toastmasters meetings. *If only* I'd been introduced to the people he'd promised, *if only* I'd been acknowledged, *if only* the executive director understood how valuable I was, then I wouldn't be so mad.

Friends, the ego wants to feel shortchanged. That's its job. My ego said, "Hey, I came through, he didn't, I am in the right." *Wrong.* Expectations = letting others dictate whether we're happy or not. I had given with my palm down: not truly giving, but *grasping.* Quid pro quo giving doesn't work. In the past when I worked with nonprofits I gave palm up. *When you give palm up you embody the spirit of service—offering, wanting nothing in return. When you give "palm down" you're grasping for personal gain.* The "palm up/palm down" value also applies to networking. Palm up = more heart-oriented interactions. Palm down = greedy grasping. Which attitude results in building relationships, providing value, and ultimately bestows benefits on both parties? You guessed it.

Not sure where to practice palm-up giving? Forgive me for promoting some of my favorite causes: The Center for Attitudinal Healing (www.healingcenter.org) provides free support services to individuals dealing with life-threatening illnesses. Over the years the charter has expanded to include services and support groups for people struggling with all sorts of crises, from the ravages of war, to the trauma of suicide, to major stress-ful life changes. Working with them is a life-enhancing experience. Love the environment and want to protect it? Check out the National Resources Defense Council (www.nrdc.org). At VolunteerMatch (www.volunteer match .org), the site that matches volunteers with non-profits across the country, you can learn about different causes, get scheduled to donate time, do "virtual volunteering" online, even make donations. It's an honor to be on their advisory board. You don't have to give money: you can give time. Organizations like VolunteerMatch make giving time insanely easy. You can also give with boundaries, and with reason—it's all okay. Just give. It feels good and will bring much joy to your life.

It's fun to be a volunteerism advocate, to encourage others to give. In the mid-1990s I received a mailing from Habitat for Humanity. Bill Gates's "high-tech house" was all over the press at the time, and his first child had recently been born. The timing was too perfect. I made a donation in the name of Jennifer Gates and sent it in. Then I e-mailed Bill and said "I just made a donation to Habitat for Humanity in Jennifer's name. May it be the first of her many charitable acts." He replied that both she and he had many charitable acts ahead. He's sure keeping his word!

The following anonymously authored Chinese proverb sums up my feelings on service and volunteering. It seems like the perfect way to end this discussion on service.

If you want happiness for an hour—take a nap.
If you want happiness for a day—go fishing.
If you want happiness for a month—get married.
If you want happiness for a year—inherit a fortune.
If you want happiness for a lifetime—help others.

HOW TO MAKE A DIFFERENCE IN THE WORLD

- Find a cause that feeds your soul. You'll know it when you find it, because you'll feel excited and uplifted at the thought of being involved. It's okay if you find multiple causes, even rotate them. I've been involved with civil rights, abused kids, homelessness, women's halfway houses, meal delivery programs, and AIDS. Each experience has stretched me in ways I could never have imagined. Learn about causes via Google, or go to www.volunteermatch.org.

- Commit to "one a week." This means giving an hour a week to a cause or an hour's worth of salary. (Or give whatever amount feels right—just give something!) You can batch up your time and/or money and give in chunks, too.

- After you make a commitment to yourself, schedule your service time to ensure it happens. Write it on your calendar, book it in your PDA, or write it on your hand—whatever it takes to make this an un-breakable date for giving. If you don't set the time aside, life will intrude and you'll lose the opportunity.

- Remember, you have a lot to give. You have time, talent, and treasure. Figure out which one feels right to give. Are you an expert in public relations, and could donate an hour a week helping a nonprofit with PR? That's donating time and talent. Would you rather write a check? That's donating treasure. It's all good.

- Get others involved. In my companies I like to match the donations given by staff members (up to a specific amount). This is fun, gets the company and the team involved in giving, and boosts morale.

COOL FREE RESOURCES

Go to www.RulesForRenegades.com and see the Personal Development section.

CONCLUSION

There's nothing more exhilarating, energizing, and absorbing than rocking your career and life. Whether you're ready to start out on your own business or just wondering what the heck to do next, I hope that this book has helped. You've read about my trials and triumphs—and seen what has worked for me and what hasn't. I trust you've found some nuggets to apply to your own life.

If you don't change the present, the future is going to look a whole lot like the past. So look around you and see where there's something that needs to be fixed, or something that's causing someone pain (that they'll pay to have cured), or something that you know you can do better than it's being done now. It might be something in your work life or something in your personal life. Look for the place where you can make a difference, be it whopping or incremental. Once you make this into a habit, you'll find that it's a lot of fun.

There are many tools in this book to help you keep things in perspective, which I didn't always do. It took my father's illness to make me stop and confront my demons of inadequacy—and to find out that there never was anything missing at all. Whatever you're feeling about yourself, remember that there's really nothing missing at all—at least nothing that you can't learn or live or find. You don't have to make it up to anybody and you don't have to prove that you're better than everybody. Consider the quote I have engraved on the back of my wristwatch:

> I am enough
> I do enough
> I have enough

Start envisioning your dream, building it until it's real and vivid and something you can depend on when the going gets rough. And when it does, it sure helps to know who you are. Go out in the world and go inside yourself at the same time. Find out why you're giving away power over your life, and figure out how to stop doing that. It always helps to be honest with yourself—but sometimes it takes a dose of bitter reality before you can see what you're really doing. Once you do see, use what you've learned here to rock rejection and finesse failure. When you know where you want to go, it becomes a lot easier to see what's keeping you from getting there.

Knowing where you're going also helps keep your eyes on the prize. When you've got that dream where you want it, start laying out the steps that will get you there. Goal setting is a powerful tool for this. The more you do it, the better you'll get at it, and the more you'll hit those marks. And when you don't hit the marks, you'll have the tools and the strength and the knowledge to take aim again, and better. We all make mistakes.

Sometimes we fall short of what we expect of ourselves. But as long as you keep moving, and keep increasing connection to yourself and others, you'll make it. In time you may find that:

Life = the people you meet + what you create together

Here's the final thought I want to leave you with . . .

DO IT ANYWAY

People are often unreasonable, illogical,
and self-centered;
Forgive them anyway.

If you are kind, people may accuse you
of selfish, ulterior motives;
Be kind anyway.

If you are successful, you will win some
false friends and some true enemies;
Succeed anyway.

If you are honest and frank,
people may cheat you;
Be honest and frank anyway.

What you spend years building, someone
could destroy overnight;
Build anyway.

If you find serenity and happiness,
they may be jealous;
Be happy anyway.

The good you do today,
people will often forget tomorrow;
Do good anyway.

Give the world the best you have,
and it may never be enough;
Give the world the best you've got anyway.

You see, in the final analysis,
it is between you and God;
It was never between you and them anyway.

—MOTHER TERESA

INDEX

Rules for Renegades Summit

As a thank you for purchasing *Rules for Renegades*, Christine Comaford-Lynch invites you and one guest to join her at the Rules for Renegades Summit free of charge. In this two day seminar you'll learn to apply the *Rules for Renegades* to your life and career. You'll leave the seminar with:

- Specific techniques to tap and apply your total talent, passion, potential, creativity

- 5 ways to increase your personal power

- 12 ways to increase the connections in your life

- 10 ways to apply your GSD to your life and career

- The Pyramid of personal relationships and how to network like the best of them

- The New Laws of Leadership and how they'll catapult your career

- The 3 ways to turn rejection on its ear—and get something great out of it

- 6 innovation acceleration techniques

- 7 steps to an irresistible pitch that executive management, financiers, customers, press won't be able to resist

- The 10 steps to getting, and staying, super motivated

ADMIT ONE

Yes! I want to Make More Money, Rock My Career, and Revel in My Individuality!

I'll register now at: www.RuleForRenegades.com/summit

I understand that admission is granted on a first come, first served basis.

ADMIT ONE

Yes! I want to Make More Money, Rock My Career, and Revel in My Individuality!

I'll register now at: www.RuleForRenegades.com/summit

I understand that admission is granted on a first come, first served basis.

The passes above are required for entry. Photocopies will not be accepted. Passes expire December 31, 2008. Attendees are responsible for their travel, lodging, meals and all other expenses.

Mighty Ventures Programs for Renegade Entrepreneurs and Intrapreneurs

CONSULTATION CALLS

Do you have a burning business issue that you need advice on? Perhaps you're launching a company or project and need help with strategy or specific steps to take, or pitfalls to avoid. Do you want to bounce some business ideas off someone with extensive startup experience? Whatever your challenge, you can discuss it with Christine. The agenda is up to you; it can be a free-form advice session, or you can shoot for a specific outcome. No matter what your individual goals are, you'll leave the call with definite "go forward" strategies and tactics that will benefit you and your company.

MENTORING & TELECLASSES

Is your business ramping up as quickly as you'd like? Could you use help in shaping your sales or marketing strategy? Identifying and securing key advisors/ board members? Mentoring is the most effective way to optimize the launch and accelerate the growth of your company. Learn sure-fire techniques to propel your business forward, differentiate your products, services, company; stand out above the crowd and attract more clients, strategic partners, market influencers. Leverage your personal expertise to tap into resources you weren't aware of, extend your skill-set and become a better executive. Create new product and service offerings to up-sell your client base. Overcome common business challenges and get advice and new approaches to staffing, funding, deal structure issues and more.

EXECUTIVE SEMINARS

Build a culture of accountability and risk-taking by bringing one of our Executive Seminars on site. We'll work with senior management to design a culture, compensation structure, team dynamic and buy-in to foster an entrepreneurial environment within your corporation. Regardless of your challenges, our Executive Seminars will cut through the issues and move the team toward growing your top line.

VENTURE SEMINARS

Once the executive team has formed the infrastructure to launch entrepreneurship internally, this seminar brings the management and staff into the fold. We'll provide everyone with tools to identify, validate and manage new ventures inside your company; ensure there are clear expectations of performance and more.

Venture Days

Once your company has set-up the infrastructure to grow new ventures and management and staff are equipped with developing new ventures, we'll come on-site to conduct a Venture Day. This is a moderated session where your staff pitches their new ventures to the executive team providing insight to new opportunities for increasing your Top Line. Each presentation follows a proscribed format to make evaluations and awards easier. This is a real attention getter and motivator as staff realizes you will make investments in their futures while promoting the overall company goals.

Pitch Critique

Nail your pitch. Pitch Critique is a one hour phone session where your business plan is critiqued. Up to five executives within your company can participate in the forum. Pitch Critique includes an assessment of your business plan's business proposition, attractiveness to financiers, and quality of sales, marketing, financial, product, staffing strategies. During the call we'll explain our findings, critique your concept, offer suggestions, and form a "go forward" strategy.

Business Plan Assessment

Business Plan Assessment is a significantly more in-depth version of Pitch Critique. If you are ready to seek financing and/or launch your company, this is the package for you. You'll receive a recording of the call for future reference. We will assess your business plan for completeness, attractiveness to financiers, and quality of sales, marketing, financials, product description and development, staffing and advisors/influencers. In a 60 minute summary of findings call, we'll explain our findings, critique your concept and offer suggestions. Within 2 weeks of the summary of findings call, we'll have a follow up call in which we'll describe pros/cons of different types of investment capital, provide high level financing strategy and be a sounding board to review your elevator pitch, presentation, and form a capital or customer acquisition strategy.

Renegade Club

This is where you find like-minded renegades who are ready to rock their careers. Learn how to implement Rules for Renegades in your own life and that of your company by applying each rule and associated worksheets with the help of fellow renegades. We provide outlines and guidance while Renegades local to you provide accountability and encouragement. What better way to rock your career than to meet and encourage renegades just like you!

E-mail contact @ mightyventures.com for more info, or call (707) 255-6246.

ake more money,

rock your career

d revel in your

individuality

make more money

ock your career,

reve

and

your individuality

make more money,

rock your career,

and revel i

your individualit